best ever activity book

best ever activity book

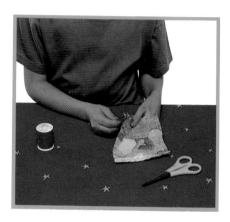

Nick Huckleberry Beak, Petra Boase,
Thomasina Smith, Jacki Wadeson

HERMES HOUSE

This edition published by Hermes House
an imprint of
Anness Publishing Limited
Hermes House
88-89 Blackfriars Road
London SE1 8HA

A CIP catalogue record for this book is available from the British Library

The activities and projects in this book were created by:
Nick Huckleberry Beak, *Clowning Around, Magic Fun and Sneaky Tricks;* Petra Boase – *Friendship Bracelets, T-shirt Painting, Modelling Fun;* Thomasina Smith – *Fancy Dress Masks, Face and Body Painting, Modelling Fun;* Jacki Wadeson – *Fabulous Hairstyles*

Publisher: Joanna Lorenz
Editor: Lyn Coutts
Photography: John Freeman, Tim Ridley
Design: Siân Keogh, Axis Design
Assistant: Christos Chrysanthou, Axis Design

© Anness Publishing Limited 1998, 2000, 2001, 2002

Previously published as *The Really Big Book of Amazing Things to Make and Do*

10 9 8 7 6 5 4 3 2 1

Please note
The level of adult supervision required will depend on the ability and age of the child, but we advise that adult supervision is always preferable and vital if the project calls for the use of sharp knives or other utensils, or involves baking items in an oven. Always keep potentially harmful tools and objects well out of the reach of young children.

Contents

Introduction

If you have always wanted to make your own friendship bracelets, create your own salt dough models or put on a magic show, then this is the book for you. There are over 120 exciting projects that you can do by following the step-by-step instructions and photographs.

Many of the projects you can do alone, but a few will require a little adult help. It may also be fun to get your friends involved in doing some of the activities with you.

You can follow a project's instructions and design to the letter, or you can modify them. You may, for example, want a picture frame to match your room or a friendship bracelet to go with a special outfit. If so, alter the colours used in the project. Likewise, you may use some of the designs as a starting point for your own truly unique creations.

The important things are that you have fun doing the projects, are careful using certain materials and equipment, and are totally happy with what you make. To help you achieve these things, read the following information.

Things you will need

All the projects in this book can be done at home in the kitchen or on a work table. Although some projects require special materials, most use everyday bits and pieces that you will already have or can find in your own home.

These are some of the basic materials and tools that you will need to get started.

Apron To prevent your clothes from getting covered in paint, face paints, modelling materials or glue, wear a smock or apron. You can also use an old, long-sleeved shirt, but wear it back to front so that you protect your clothing.

Card and paper Brightly coloured and plain white card and paper are needed for some projects. Though it may sometimes be necessary to buy large sheets of special card or paper, many projects can be completed using recycled cereal packets or leftover pieces of paper.

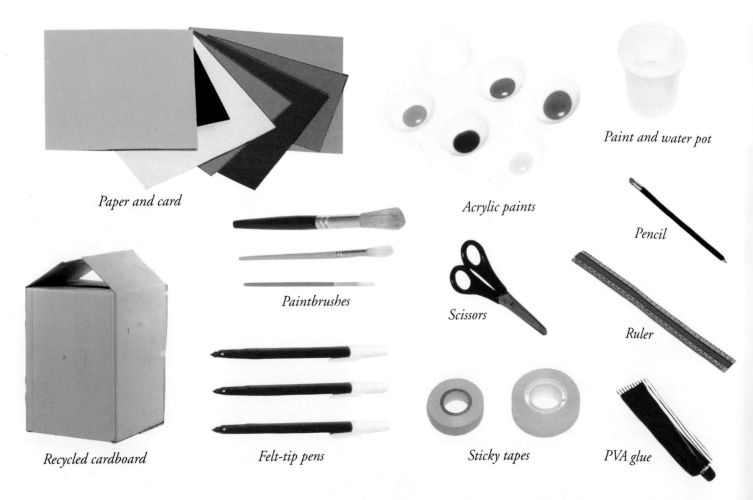

Paper and card

Acrylic paints

Paint and water pot

Pencil

Paintbrushes

Scissors

Ruler

Recycled cardboard

Felt-tip pens

Sticky tapes

PVA glue

Cardboard Some projects use thick or corrugated cardboard to make models. Cutting up old, empty boxes is a good source of cardboard.

Felt-tip pens These are always good to use on paper or card. Some felt-tip pens have fine points, others broad. Choose the one most suitable for the project.

Paint and water pot This is a special lidded pot that will not spill its contents even if knocked over. You will need this for mixing your paints and cleaning your paintbrushes.

Paintbrushes Paintbrushes come in many different shapes and sizes. You will need fine, pointed paintbrushes as well as thick or flat-ended paintbrushes for covering large areas.

Paints There are lots of different kinds of paints, and it is important to use the sort that is best for the job you are doing. Sometimes pale, watery paint is perfect but at other times you need strong, bright paints that will cover printing or pictures on recycled paper or packaging.

The paint recommended for decorating most surfaces is acrylic paint. This can be mixed with water to make it runny, or used straight from the tube, pot or palette to give bold colours. Acrylic paints can be bought in stationery shops and art and craft shops. You can also use poster paints.

Pencil For planning a design or for making feint or removable marks on an item, use a lead pencil. A soft lead pencil is also necessary when making templates and stencils. Have a rubber on hand, to remove any mistakes.

PVA glue This glue has many other names. You may know it as white glue, school glue or woodworking glue. It is a water-based glue. This means that your hands and glue brush will come clean under the tap. PVA glue is white, so that you can see where you have applied it, but it becomes clear when it dries. You can apply glue with a brush or glue spreader.

This glue sticks most things together – paper, cardboard, wood, cellophane, cloth and plastic. It is great for making papier-mâché and for sticking glitter to a surface. To get paint to adhere to a plastic surface, first mix a little PVA glue into the paint colour.

You can make a varnish by mixing three parts of PVA glue with one part water. Paint this on to finished models to give them a smooth, shiny surface.

Use an apron or old shirt to protect your clothing.

Ruler You will need a ruler to make accurate measurements and to draw straight lines. It needs to be marked in centimetres (cm) and millimetres (mm) or feet (ft) and inches (in).

Scissors There are two different types of scissors. There are those with pointed blades and those with rounded blades. Rounded blades, or safety scissors, are much safer to use, but they may not be strong enough to cut thick card or cardboard. If you need to use pointed scissors, ask permission first or ask an adult for help. For some projects you can choose to use fancy scissors. The blades on these scissors have zigzag or wavy edges that give cut paper a decorative edge.

Sticky tapes Throughout this book a variety of sticky tapes is used. For joining lightweight items, you can use ordinary, clear sticky tape. To join card or cardboard, you will need a stronger tape like masking tape. Masking tape can be removed and it can also be painted over. Electrical tape, or insulating tape, is very strong and it comes in lots of bright colours so it can also be used to decorate items.

If you cannot get hold of certain items for a project, then look around the home for a substitute. You never know, your substitute material may even look better than the original!

Recycling materials

Everyone's house is full of bits and pieces that can be recycled and used to make the projects in this book. Store your trove of recycled treasure in a large, empty box. Once you start making things, you will be watching out to see what can be saved from the dustbin and made into a gift. The sorts of things to look out for are:

- wrapping paper
- ribbon and string
- beads and buttons
- milk or juice cartons
- greetings cards
- empty tins with a smooth, rounded edge
- magazines and newspapers
- plastic drinks bottles
- remnants of fabric
- plastic bottle tops
- yoghurt pots

- lightweight card boxes used for food packaging
- boxes made of corrugated card
- cardboard tubes
- egg boxes
- lolly sticks
- foil pie cases
- corks
- shells
- cotton reels
- sweet wrappers

Always wash milk or juice containers and yoghurt pots in warm, soapy water before storing them away for later use.

It is important to know when to stop collecting. If you have enough recycled packaging to fill your box, then stop collecting and start making things! Do not forget to recycle any scraps of paper or card left over from a project – they are bound to come in handy.

How to remove labels

Fill a washing-up bowl or basin with warm water and soak the bottle or container in the water for about 10 minutes. If the label is still not loose, soak again and use a scouring pad to help remove the label.

Flattening and cutting up boxes

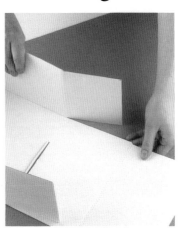 

1 Remove any sticky tape that is holding the box together. Press the box flat.

2 Cut the box into sections following the fold lines and using a pair of scissors.

Discard any pieces that are too damaged or creased to be of use. Your card will keep best if stored flat.

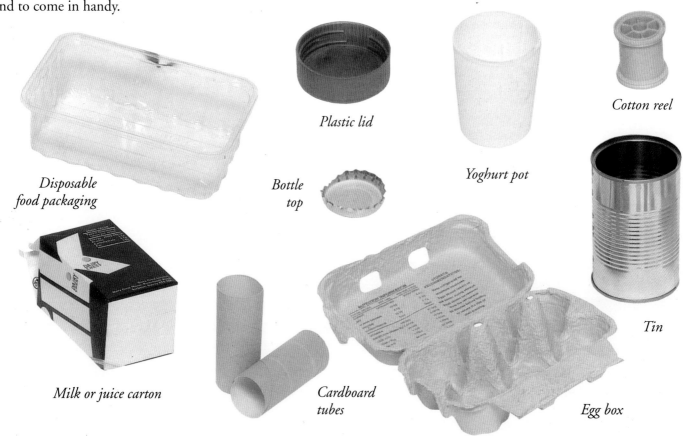

Disposable food packaging

Plastic lid

Yoghurt pot

Cotton reel

Bottle top

Tin

Milk or juice carton

Cardboard tubes

Egg box

Getting started

1. Carefully read through the list of materials you will need.

2. Read through the instructions and look at the photographs so that you have a clear idea of what you will be doing.

3. Collect everything you will need for the project. Ask permission before you borrow anything.

4. Protect your clothing with an apron or old shirt, and cover your work surface with newspaper or wipe-clean plastic.

5. Lay out all the materials on your work surface.

6. Have on hand a damp cloth to wipe up any spills and to clean your hands.

7. When cutting materials with a knife, place a chopping board underneath.

8. Follow the steps in order and allow time for paint or glue to dry before going on to the next step.

9. Ask an adult for help if suggested in the instructions. An adult should always supervise use of sharp tools and the oven.

10. Do not rush. Give yourself plenty of time in which to create something really special.

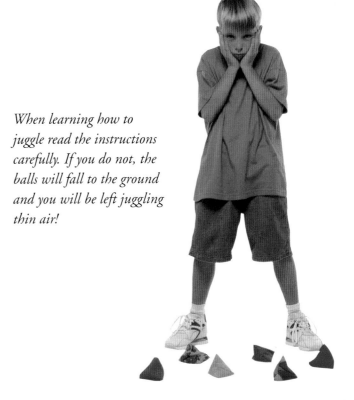

When learning how to juggle read the instructions carefully. If you do not, the balls will fall to the ground and you will be left juggling thin air!

Weighing and measuring

The ingredients in recipes are measured in grams (g) and millilitres (ml) and in ounces (oz) and fluid ounces (fl oz). Dimensions are measured in centimetres (cm), millimetres (mm) and metres (m). Imperial equivalents are given in inches (in), feet (ft) and yards (yd).

It is very important that you choose either metric or imperial measurements when weighing or measuring. Never mix the two units. Use either centimetres or inches, for example, not a combination of the two.

Finishing up

When you have finished, always clear up and put away all your things and return any items that you have borrowed. Keep any remnants or scraps that may come in handy for future craft projects.

Looking after your materials

❖ Save any left-over modelling materials by storing them in air-tight containers or sealed bags. Unused salt dough should be wrapped in plastic food wrap and stored in a refrigerator.

❖ Store paper, card or cardboard flat or rolled up and secured with a rubber band.

❖ Take great care of your paintbrushes by using them gently. If you move your paintbrushes in one direction, this will keep the bristles smooth and make them last longer. Always wash your paintbrushes and dry them with a paper towel after you have used them. Store them flat so that the bristles remain straight.

❖ Replace the lids and caps on felt-tip pens, tubes or bottles of glue, palettes of fabric paint and containers of glitter. This will prevent the item drying out or spilling.

Cover the work surface with sheets of newspaper or wipe-clean plastic. They prevent paint or glue staining the work surface and make cleaning-up much easier!

Basic Techniques

Cutting out a circle

It is difficult to cut a circle out of a thick card or cardboard. The best way to do it is to ask an adult to stab a small hole in the centre of the circle using the point of a sharp pair of scissors. Then make several small cuts outwards from the hole to the edge of the circle. You will now be able to cut around the edge of the circle quickly and easily.

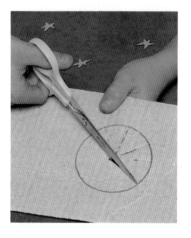 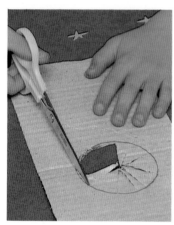

Painting straight lines

Stick lengths of masking tape along a drawn line on the item. Press the tape firmly into position. Apply the paint so that it runs a little over the edge of the tape. When the paint is dry, carefully pull off the masking tape.

Painting plastic

To make paint stick to plastic surfaces, add a small amount of PVA glue to the paint and mix well. If the mixture is too thick, add a little water.

Painting round objects

To stop round objects rolling around while they are being painted, rest them in a holder. Plastic plant pots, cups and egg boxes make excellent holders. Choose a holder that is the right size for the item you are painting.

Varnishing

PVA glue can be used to make a varnish that will give finished projects a smooth, shiny finish. To make the varnish, mix three parts PVA glue to one part water in a bowl. The varnish is white when wet, but clear when dry. Apply the varnish gently on to dry surfaces with a brush.

Mixing paint colours

You do not need lots of paint colours to complete the projects. All you need are the primary colours – red, blue and yellow – and black and white. From these colours you can make all the colours of the rainbow.

Mix red and blue to make purple

Mix red and yellow to make orange

Mix blue and yellow to make green

By varying the amount of each primary colour used when mixing a colour, you can make different tones of purple, orange and green. To make a colour lighter or darker, add white or black. Always add white or black a little at a time until you get exactly the colour you want.

A paint palette is very useful for mixing small quantities of paint. Use a paint pot or empty yoghurt pot to mix large quantities of paint.

Tips for mixing paint colours

❖ If you need a large quantity of a colour but have to mix colours together to make it, start out by mixing just a small amount. Try to remember as you are making the colour, which colours you used and in what proportions. When you have created the right colour, then you can go on to make the large quantity.

❖ A paint palette is perfect for mixing small amounts of colour. It is best to mix large amounts of paint in a paint pot, empty yoghurt pot or on the lid of an unwanted plastic container.

❖ Change the water in the water pot regularly. If you add dirty water to a paint, it will make the colour darker.

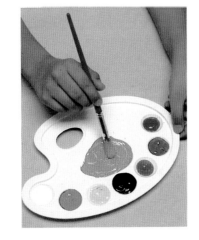

Safety first!

❖ Keep all small items, sharp tools, glues, modelling materials and any other dangerous items well out of the reach of young children.

❖ Always ask an adult to help you light or turn on the oven or stove. An adult should also carry out or supervise you when items are being put into or being removed from an oven. Wear oven gloves when handling hot items. Never touch a baking tray or the baked items until they are cold.

❖ Ask permission from an adult before borrowing or using any type of electrical appliance.

❖ Check with an adult before using any type of make-up remover, cream or cleanser on your face or body. Face paint can be washed off with mild soap and water.

❖ You must never use acrylic or poster paints, felt-tip pens, crayons, craft glues or other stationery items on your face. They may cause a rash or irritation.

❖ When making holes in card or other materials with a pair of scissors, always make sure the blades of the scissors are closed and that you point the tip of the blades away from you. Never put your hand under the item while you are making a hole in it.

❖ When cutting any material that might fly up into your eyes, wear some protection over your eyes. You can buy inexpensive safety goggles from a hardware shop, but swimming goggles make a good substitute.

❖ When using glue, paint or glitter try not to touch your face or rub your eyes. These materials can cause irritation. Wash your hands after using these materials.

❖ Read the instructions on any packaging before using its contents. This is especially important when using face paints, fabric paints and some modelling materials.

Tracing a Template

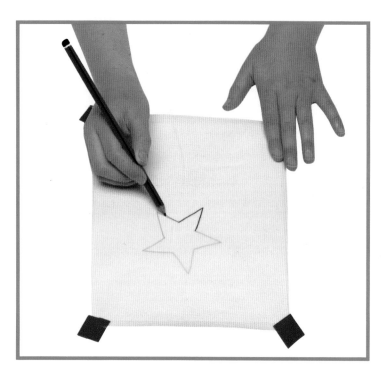

1 Place a piece of tracing paper over the template and secure it at the corners with tape. Carefully draw around the shape using a soft lead pencil.

2 Take the tracing paper off the template and turn the paper over. Rub over the traced image with the pencil on the reverse side of the tracing paper.

3 Place the tracing paper on a piece of card, with the traced outline face up. Draw firmly over the outline to transfer the template on to the card.

4 Cut out your template. To use a template on paper, card or fabric, simply draw around the shape with a pencil, felt-tip pen or fabric marker pen.

Making a Stencil

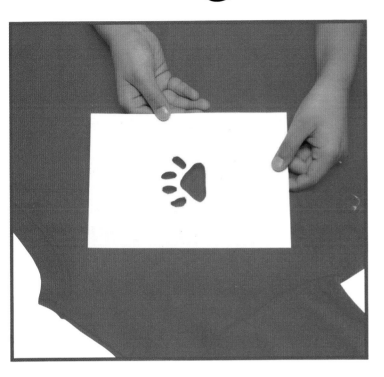

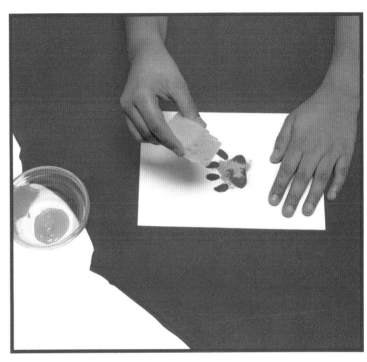

1 Follow steps 1 to 3 of Tracing a Template to make a tracing of the outline. Use scissors to snip into the middle of the outline. Cut out the stencil following the outline.

2 Place the stencil on to the paper, card or fabric to be decorated. Lightly press a dry sponge into paint or fabric paint. Then dab the sponge on to the stencil.

A stencil lets you repeat a design over and over again. These paw prints were made using a stencil dabbed with brown paint.

3 Lift the stencil off the decorated item. To keep printing the stencil, repeat steps 2 and 3. Check that there is no paint on the back of the stencil before continuing to print.

Modelling Fun

Petra Boase
Thomasina Smith

Introduction

Modelling is not just about making sculptures of animals or people, it is also about creating useful things like pots and plates. Even jewellery can be fashioned from modelling material and then decorated. In ancient cultures, nearly everything needed for cooking or for serving food was made from clay. The clay was then baked to make it hard. The ancient Greeks used clay to make beautiful pots, called urns, in which they collected water and stored food. Many of these pots were decorated with patterns or pictures and then painted.

Types of modelling materials

In Modelling Fun, we use several different types of modelling material. There are projects that use a material that hardens when baked in the oven, a special drying material that hardens without baking, and a plastic type that remains soft so that it can be used over and over again.

There are also projects made with salt dough. This can be made at home by using the recipe that follows. All the other types of modelling materials can be bought in toy, craft or hobby shops.

Always store your modelling materials in sealed plastic bags or airtight containers. This will keep them clean and ready for future use. Drying modelling material will harden if it is left out in the open air.

What you can make

Your friends will be astounded when they see the weird and wonderful things you have made using the projects in Modelling Fun. There is a Grinning Cat, a Snappy Crocodile and a friendly dinosaur. There are also Heart and Star Rings and a Heart Throb Bracelet, Coiled Pot and Plate, a pirate's Treasure Chest and a Space Rocket. The project that will doubly impress your friends is the Spotty Clock. Not only does its salt dough clock face look terrific, but it tells the time!

After making a few of the models shown here, why not design some of your own? You could create some more characters like Wonder Boy and write a play about their adventures. Once you have learned the knack of making animals, you could create your own miniature wildlife park or farmyard. There is no end to the amount of crafty modelling fun you can have.

Safety

There are a few rules to follow when preparing and baking your models.

1. To cut a piece of modelling material, use a butter knife or the bladed end of a plastic modelling tool. Modelling materials are soft – there is no need for sharp cutting utensils.

2. Always ask an adult to turn on the oven and set the temperature. An adult should supervise placing the baking tray into the oven and removing it. When doing these things and transferring the baked items to a cooling rack, always wear a pair of oven gloves. Do not touch the baked items until they have had time to cool down.

3. Keep hot baking trays and modelling materials out of reach of young children.

Materials and equipment

Acrylic paint This is a water-based paint that comes in a range of vibrant colours.

Baking modelling material This material hardens when it is baked in an oven. It comes in a range of colours. Always read the instructions on the packet.

Baking tray You will need a baking tray when using baking modelling material.

Biscuit cutters These are used to cut interesting shapes from modelling material. Use either plastic or metal ones.

Chopping board Use a plastic chopping board to protect tabletops when modelling. Wash thoroughly after use.

Cooling rack After the salt dough has baked in the oven, place it on a cooling rack to cool before painting.

Drying modelling material This white or terracotta modelling material will harden in about 24 hours without baking. Always read the instructions on the packet.

Fine sandpaper Before the baked salt dough is painted, rough edges are smoothed by rubbing sandpaper over them.

Modelling tool The most useful modelling tool has one pointy end and one flat end. This tool can be used for carving and sculpting.

Oven gloves These must be worn when removing a baking tray from the oven and when handling hot salt dough models.

Parchment paper This prevents the salt dough sticking to the baking tray when it is baking.

Plastic modelling material This inexpensive and reusable material comes in lots of bright colours. It does not harden, so the models are less permanent.

PVA glue This is strong glue for joining surfaces but it can also be mixed with water to make a varnish for your models.

Rolling pin This is for rolling salt dough flat. Before using, dust the rolling pin with flour to stop the dough sticking.

Tall, thick glass Use a thick glass for rolling out baking, drying or plastic modelling material. Do not use a wooden rolling pin – these materials will stick to it.

Varnish If you do not want to make a varnish with PVA glue, you can buy ready-made varnish from art and craft shops.

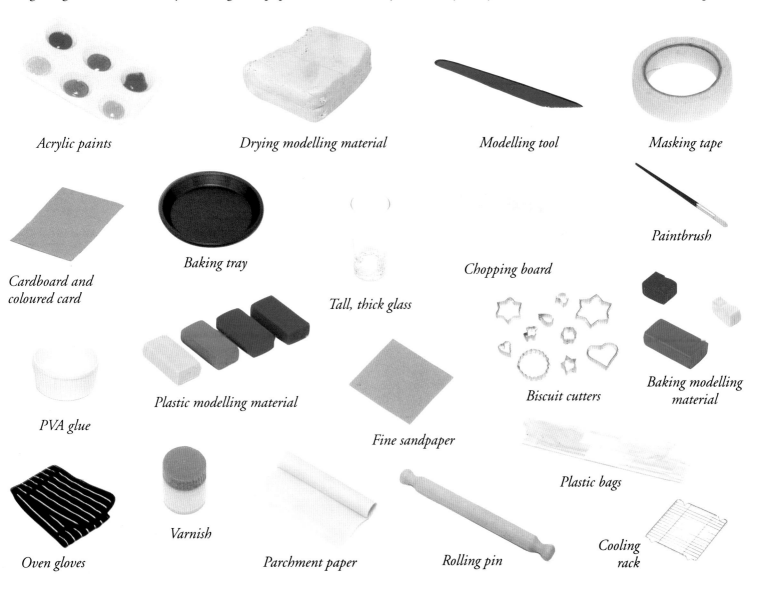

Acrylic paints

Drying modelling material

Modelling tool

Masking tape

Paintbrush

Baking tray

Cardboard and coloured card

Tall, thick glass

Chopping board

Plastic modelling material

Biscuit cutters

Baking modelling material

PVA glue

Fine sandpaper

Plastic bags

Oven gloves

Varnish

Parchment paper

Rolling pin

Cooling rack

Basic Techniques

These basic techniques apply to baking, drying and plastic modelling materials.

To soften modelling material, hold it in your hands. Their warmth will soften it and make it easy to model.

To roll out modelling material, apply even pressure and use a thick glass to get a smooth surface of the right thickness.

Shaping materials

To shape modelling materials you can use your hands to make round or oval balls, and snakes and sausages. The secret to modelling with your hands is to be patient and to mould the material gently. If you press too firmly, ball shapes will become blobs and snakes will be uneven. To make textures, smooth joins or to cut modelling materials, it is best to use a modelling tool. For small, detail work like adding features to a face, a cocktail stick is perfect. You can also shape modelling material by moulding it on to a plate or around a cup.

Attaching limbs

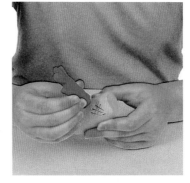

One way of securely fixing limbs to a body is to score lots of fine lines on both pieces. Press the pieces together and smooth the join using a modelling tool.

An alternative method is to make a hole in the body with the thin end of a modelling tool. Shape the end of the limb into a point and push it into the hole firmly.

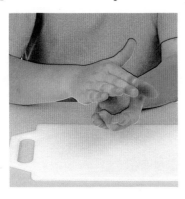

To make snake and sausage shapes, roll the modelling material back and forth under the palms of your hands and fingers. Move your hands along the material to make it even.

To make a round ball, gently roll a piece of modelling material between your flattened palms. Cut the ball in half with a modelling tool or butter knife to make dome shapes.

Keeping colours separate

To stop plastic modelling material colours being mixed together, tape sheets of white paper on to your work surface or chopping board. Roll or model only one colour of material on each sheet. After finishing a model, put the paper aside and use it the next time you use the same colour.

How to Make Salt Dough

For some of the projects you need to make a quantity of salt dough.

YOU WILL NEED THESE MATERIALS AND TOOLS

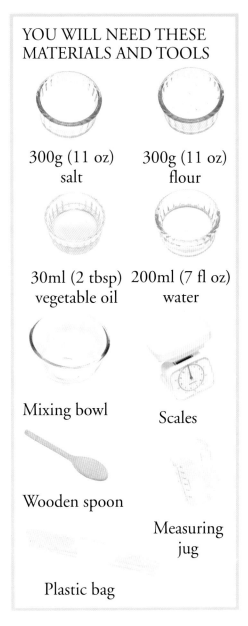

300g (11 oz) salt

300g (11 oz) flour

30ml (2 tbsp) vegetable oil

200ml (7 fl oz) water

Mixing bowl

Scales

Wooden spoon

Measuring jug

Plastic bag

1 Use the scales to weigh the correct amount of flour and salt. Put the flour and salt in the bowl. Mix them together using the wooden spoon.

2 Measure 200ml (7 fl oz) of water in a measuring jug. Pour the water gradually over the flour and salt and mix well.

3 Pour the oil over the mixture and mix it in well. When all the oil has been absorbed, remove the dough from the bowl and place on a clean surface that has been sprinkled with flour.

4 Knead the dough with your hands until it is firm, then put it in a plastic bag or wrap it in plastic food wrap. Place the dough in the refrigerator for 30 minutes before you use it.

Handy hint

If you do not use all the salt dough you have made, store it in an airtight container or a plastic bag and put it in the refrigerator. When you want to use it again, simply sprinkle it with flour and knead it. This will soften the salt dough and make it easy to work with.

Remember that models made with salt dough will be fragile, so handle them with care.

Wiggly Snake Frame

Snakes alive! This fun picture or mirror frame will catch everyone's attention. It is bound to be a great hit. Hiss!

Handy hint

The length of the snakes will vary according to the size of your frame. Do not forget that you will have to make two long and two short snakes for a rectangular picture frame.

YOU WILL NEED THESE MATERIALS AND TOOLS

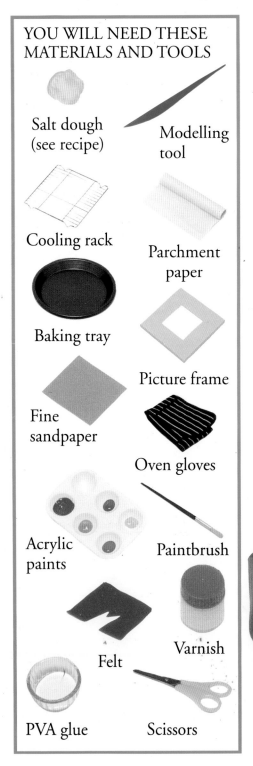

Salt dough (see recipe)

Modelling tool

Cooling rack

Parchment paper

Baking tray

Picture frame

Fine sandpaper

Oven gloves

Acrylic paints

Paintbrush

Felt

Varnish

PVA glue

Scissors

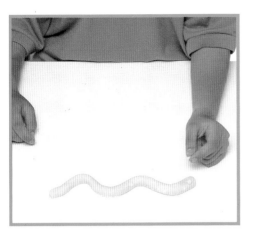

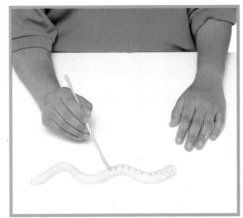

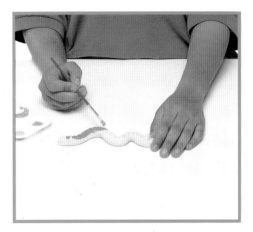

1 Roll out a piece of salt dough and bend it into a wiggly shape. Roll two small balls of salt dough for the eyes and attach them to one end of the snake. Make three more snakes in exactly the same way.

2 Decorate each snake with spots, zigzags or stripes using the modelling tool. Place the snakes on a piece of parchment paper on a baking tray and bake them for about four hours at 120°C/250°F/Gas ½.

3 Ask an adult to remove the hardened snakes from the oven with a pair of oven gloves and to place them on a cooling rack. When cool, lightly rub the snakes with sandpaper before painting and varnishing them.

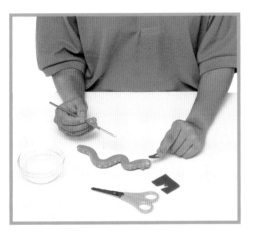

4 To make a tongue for each snake, use scissors to cut Y-shaped pieces of coloured felt. Glue a tongue to the underside of each snake's head. The forked section should protrude from the front of the head.

5 Use a pencil and ruler to draw a chequer-board pattern on to the front and sides of the frame. Paint the frame using two colours, as shown. To finish, glue the snakes on, one on each edge of the frame.

Daisy frame

If snakes gives you the shivers, then decorate your frame with salt dough daisies. Follow the steps for Wiggly Snake Frame, but use biscuit cutters to make the daisies and the centres.

This cheerful picture frame will add colour to any shelf or wall. You could paint the flowers and decorate the frame to match your room. These daisy shapes would look great on round or oval frames, too.

Space Rocket

This rocket is made using a rocket-shaped cardboard base covered with colourful plastic modelling material. Not only does this method make the model stronger, it means that you can be more inventive when you design your own deep-Space explorer.

YOU WILL NEED THESE MATERIALS AND TOOLS

Coloured pencil

Thick cardboard

Scissors

Ruler

Masking tape

Chopping board

Modelling tool

Tall, thick glass

Plastic modelling material (white, black, purple, green, orange, yellow)

'Mission control to Space Rocket commander, are you ready for blast off? We are starting countdown.'

1 On a piece of thick cardboard, use the pencil to draw two tongue-like shapes 20cm x 8cm (8in x 3in). On one of the shapes mark a 3mm (^{1}/$_{16}$in) wide slit, as shown. On the other, draw semi-circular fins on either side.

2 Cut out both pieces and the slit. Slot the finned piece into the slit so that the rocket will stand upright. If the model leans to one side, trim the base to straighten it. Fasten the joins with masking tape.

3 Roll out pieces of plastic modelling material in different colours. Mould these firmly on to the card base, pinching the joins together securely. Use the modelling tool to trim the edges and draw markings.

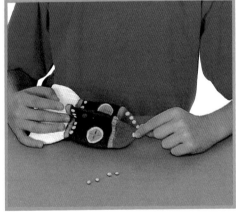

4 When the rocket is covered with modelling material, press on flattened balls of modelling material to make windows and rivets.

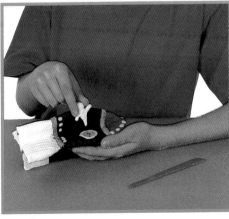

5 Mould an astronaut from white material. Make a hole in a window and press the astronaut into the hole.

Once you have constructed your first Space Rocket, you can go on to design a whole fleet of rockets, Space labs or alien Space ships. It is best not to make the cardboard base too large because the amount of modelling material needed to cover it will keep your craft Earthbound.

Sun and Star Pot

This pot is made from slabs of modelling material. The slabs are joined by smoothing the inside seams with a modelling tool. When the pot is complete, smooth the outside seams. This pot is ideal for storing small valuables. To make a nest of pots, make two more pots – one smaller and one larger than your Sun and Star Pot.

YOU WILL NEED THESE MATERIALS AND TOOLS

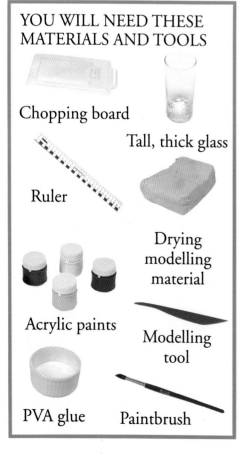

Chopping board

Tall, thick glass

Ruler

Drying modelling material

Acrylic paints

Modelling tool

PVA glue   Paintbrush

24

1 Roll a large slab of material until it is 5mm (¹/₄in) thick. Use an up-turned glass to cut out two circles. Cut out two strips, one 25cm x 5cm (10in x 2in) and one 25cm x 2cm (10in x ³/₄in).

2 To make the lid, roll out one of the circles until it is 5mm (¹/₄in) wider than the other circle. Score around the side of the lid before pressing on the narrow strip. Bind the edges together.

3 Score the side of the remaining circle and carefully wrap the wider strip of material around it. Support the sides of the pot as you bind the edges together and smooth the joins.

Painting tips

❖ Paint the inside and outside of the pot first. While this is drying, paint the top and the bottom of the lid yellow. Decorate the pot with stars and then go on to complete the lid with the blue and green paint. To finish, paint stars on the lid.

❖ To make the stars and moons really shine, sprinkle gold or silver glitter on to the wet paint.

❖ If you are into astrology, you could paint star signs around the side of the pot or on to the lid.

4 Press an upturned glass on to rolled out material to make the outline of a circle. Into the centre, place a small circle of material. Carve the Sun's rays around it using the modelling tool.

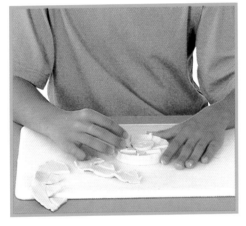

5 Cut out the Sun with the modelling tool and position it on the flat, upper surface of the lid. Place the lid on the up-turned glass to dry. Allow the pot and the lid to dry for 12 hours before turning them over to dry for further 12 hours.

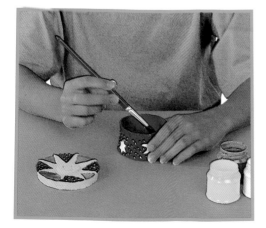

6 Paint and decorate the insides and outsides of the pot and lid. When dry, apply a varnish of 8 parts PVA glue to 1 part water.

Spotty Clock

Watch time tick by on this Spotty Clock. The only special items you require to make this working clock are a pair of clock hands and clock workings. These can be bought in specialist hobby and craft shops. Check which size battery is required and read the assembly instructions for the kit carefully.

YOU WILL NEED THESE MATERIALS AND TOOLS

Salt dough (see recipe)

Rolling pin

Modelling tool

Baking tray

Oven gloves

Cooling rack

Varnish

Fine sandpaper

Paintbrush

Acrylic paints

Parchment paper

Round pastry cutter

Clock hands and workings

1 Roll out a piece of salt dough to 1cm (¹/₂in) thick. Place a plate on the dough and cut round it. Find the centre of the circle and make a small hole. Make sure the clock workings will go through this hole.

2 Roll out another piece of salt dough to about 5mm (¹/₄in) thick and cut out 12 circles of dough with the round pastry cutter. Stick four circles of dough on to the clock face with a dab of water to mark 12, 3, 6 and 9. Use the remaining circles to decorate the clock face. Bake the clock face on a baking tray lined with parchment paper for about five hours at 120°C/250°F/Gas ½.

3 Ask an adult to remove the hardened salt dough from the oven with oven gloves and place it on a cooling rack. When cool, smooth the edge of the clock face with sandpaper. Paint the clock face a light colour before painting the circles in contrasting colours. It is good idea to paint the circles for 12, 3, 6 and 9 in the same colour. Paint a line around the edge of the clock face.

4 Mark the four points of the clock face by painting on the numbers. When dry, apply a coat of varnish. Attach the clock hands and workings following the instructions on the kit.

This is just one way of decorating the clock face. You may like to use stars, squares, diamonds, hearts or flower shapes. These shapes and many more can be made with fancy biscuit cutters. It is important that the shapes are not too large or too thick. If they are too thick, the hands will not be able to move around the clock face.

Snappy Crocodile

This fantastic crocodile is made from a special modelling clay that hardens when baked in the oven. This means that Snappy will be flashing its fangs at passers-by for years to come. Just like a real crocodile, Snappy has pointy teeth and stays cool by keeping its mouth open.

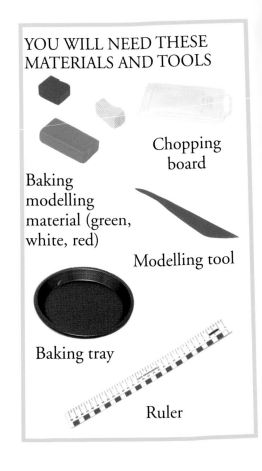

YOU WILL NEED THESE MATERIALS AND TOOLS

Chopping board

Baking modelling material (green, white, red)

Modelling tool

Baking tray

Ruler

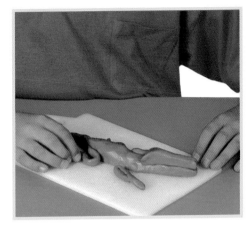

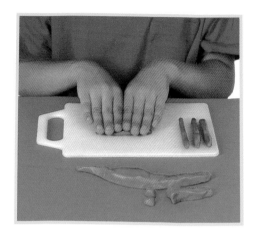

1 Roll one sausage 15cm (6in) long, another 6cm (2½in) long and four more 5cm (2in) long. Roll two balls for the eyes. Shape the two large sausages to make Snappy's body and upper jaw.

2 Press the jaw and legs into position. Bend the back legs to look like those of a real crocodile. Fold the front legs so that they are thicker at the top. Smooth the joins with your fingers.

3 Press a ball of white material on to each of the small green balls. Press a little red material on top to complete the eyes. Position the eyes to cover the join between the jaw and body.

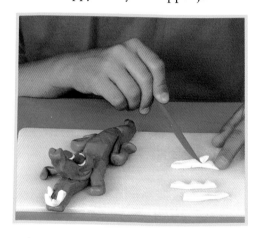

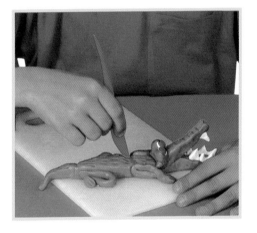

4 Cut four rectangular strips of white modelling material. Carefully carve small triangles from the strips to make pointed and jagged teeth. Position them neatly along Snappy's jaws. Press them firmly into position.

5 Use the modelling tool to mark scales on the crocodile's back. Place your masterpiece on a baking tray. Ask an adult to put it in the oven and to bake it according to the instructions on the packet.

Toothy reminder

Snappy's brilliant white teeth could act as a reminder for you to clean your teeth. To transform Snappy into the most ferocious toothbrush holder in the world, just make sure that when modelling its mouth the opening is wide enough to fit a toothbrush.

Did you know that crocodiles can grow to a length of 6m (20ft)? But do not try to make a life-size Snappy model because it will never fit in the oven!

Coiled Plate

This plate is for decoration only! Remember to use an ovenproof plate for the mould.

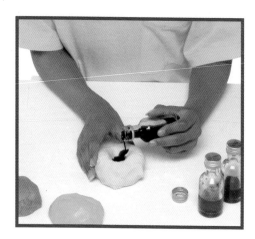

1 Divide the dough into three balls. Make a well in the centre of each ball and add three drops of food colouring to each. Each ball will be a different colour. Knead them on a floured surface to spread the colouring evenly. Lightly oil the ovenproof plate.

2 Roll the balls of dough into long, thin sausages. Place the end of one sausage at the centre of the ovenproof plate and coil it around. Join the next sausage to the end of the first piece and continue coiling. Do the same with the remaining sausage.

3 Decorate the edge and centre of the plate with small balls of coloured dough. Bake the plate in the oven for six hours at 120°C/ 250°F/Gas ½. Ask an adult to remove the hardened salt dough from the oven with oven gloves and transfer to a cooling rack.

YOU WILL NEED THESE MATERIALS AND TOOLS

Food colouring (3 different colours)

Vegetable oil

Cooling rack

Salt dough (see recipe)

Varnish

Ovenproof plate

Paintbrush

Oven gloves

When cool, give your Coiled Plate a shiny finish by applying a coat of varnish.

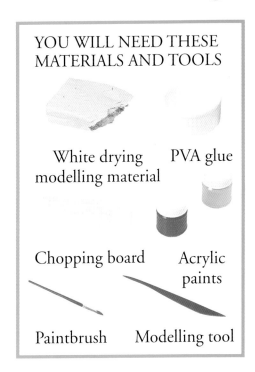

Snake Pot

This little storage pot looks like a sleeping snake curled around on itself.

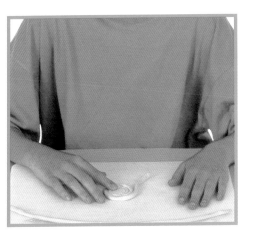

1 Cut three pieces of drying modelling material and roll each into a snake. Make each one as long as possible but not too thin. Tightly coil one of the snakes into a flat circle. This will be the base of the pot. If there are any gaps, gently press them together. Bind the joins with the modelling tool.

2 Build the walls of the pot by coiling a snake on top of the outer edge of the base. Smooth the ridges on the inside of the pot. Continue coiling with the second snake. When you have finished, shape the end to make the snake's face. Use the modelling tool to carve a pattern around the edge.

Handy hint

If you want to make a larger coil pot to use as a pencil holder, roll the snakes a little thicker. If you need more snakes to complete your pot, bind the snakes together and keep coiling.

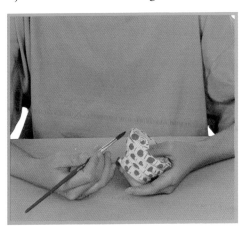

3 Allow the pot to dry for about 12 hours on each side before painting it yellow with red spots. To finish, apply a varnish made of 8 parts PVA glue and 1 part water.

The Snake Pot is the perfect place to store small treasures or even pocket money. No one would dare touch it for fear of disturbing the sleeping snake!

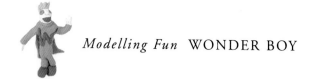

Wonder Boy

Like all great superheroes, Wonder Boy wears a dashing cape and has superhuman powers. You could build a whole story world about Wonder Boy's thrilling adventures from modelling material. Your hero could save a city of skyscrapers from the rampages of monsters and dinosaurs!

YOU WILL NEED THESE MATERIALS AND TOOLS

Modelling tool

Chopping board

Plastic modelling material (green, orange, white, red, yellow)

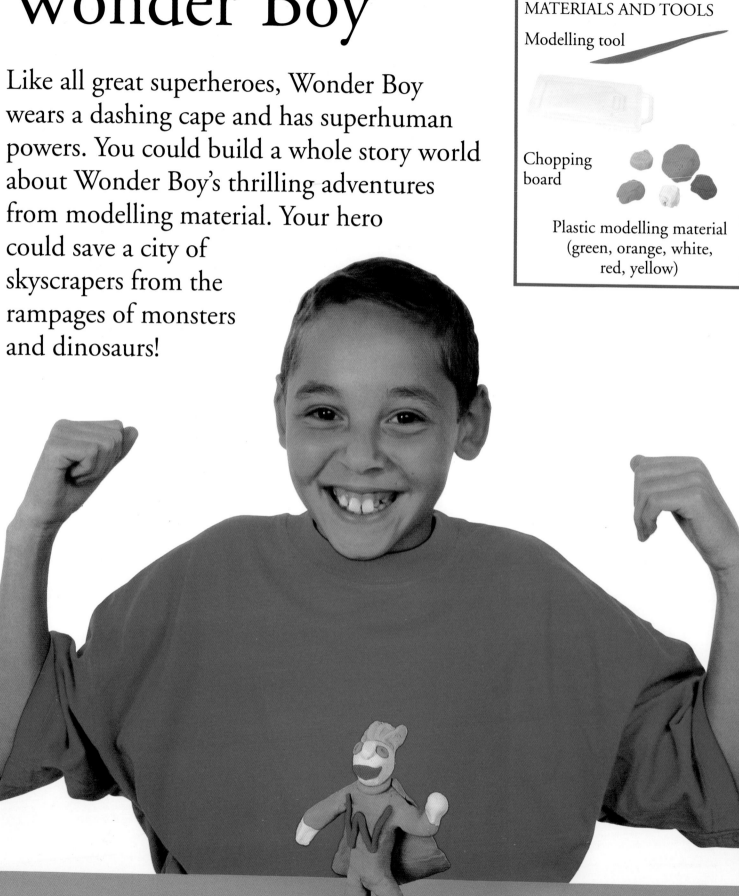

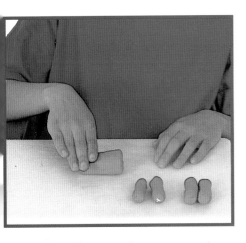

1 Roll out four small sausages and one large sausage from green modelling material. The large sausage will be the superhero's body, so it should be narrow at the top and wide at the bottom.

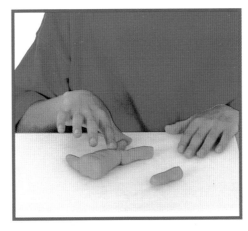

2 Firmly press the four small sausages on to the body to make the legs and arms of Wonder Boy. Use your fingers to carefully bind and smooth the joins. Make sure that your model can stand.

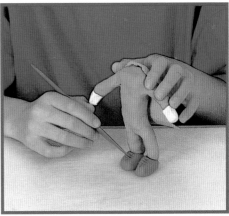

3 Roll out orange modelling material and shape it to make a cloak. Shape two white balls to make fists, and two red balls to make a pair of shoes. Press the pieces into position and decorate.

4 To make the face, roll a ball of white material. Use scraps of modelling material to make the eyes, mouth and nose. Carve a piece of yellow material for the hair and press it into position.

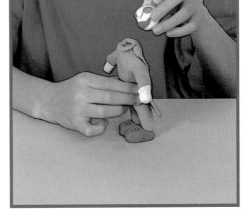

5 Roll a thin, short sausage of green material, shape it into a small circle and position it where the head will go. Press the head firmly on to the body and smooth the join. Lay Wonder Boy gently on to his back.

If you want to give your superhero a different name, do not forget to alter the letter on the model's chest. In place of a letter, you can use a star, lightning flash or other symbol.

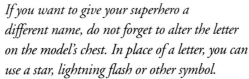

6 Roll out a snake of red material. Press it on to Wonder Boy's chest in the shape of the letter 'W'.

Family of Pigs

These three little pigs would make lovely ornaments for a shelf or window ledge. They would be the perfect gift for someone who collects models of pigs. Sows can have up to ten piglets in a litter, so make as many as you like!

YOU WILL NEED THESE MATERIALS AND TOOLS

Salt dough (see recipe)

Cocktail stick

Parchment paper

Oven gloves

Fine sandpaper

Baking tray

Paintbrush

Acrylic paints

Cooling rack

Varnish

These pigs have been painted pale pink, but you could paint them any colour you like or even decorate them in wild patterns. You may even like to give each pig a name that could be painted on to the side of its body.

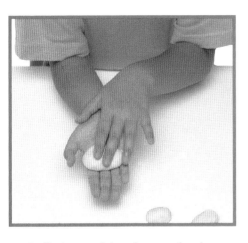

1 Roll pieces of dough to make three oval shapes of different sizes. Shape one end of each oval into a pig's face and use a cocktail stick to mark eyes and nostrils. Attach two small triangles of dough on to each head for the ears.

2 Roll a small piece of salt dough into a long strip for each pig's tail and stick one on to the back of each pig with a dab of water. Gently bend it into a coil shape. Place the pigs on a baking tray lined with parchment paper.

3 Form 12 stumpy, round legs from small balls of salt dough. Try to make the legs the same size. Place them on the baking tray with the pigs' bodies. Ask an adult to bake them in the oven for five hours at 120°C/250°F/Gas ½.

! SAFETY

Always ask an adult to help you set the oven temperature. Wear oven gloves when placing the baking tray in the oven and when removing it. A pair of tongs or an egg slice will make it easy and safe to transfer hot items from the baking tray on to the cooling rack. Allow plenty of time for your models to cool.

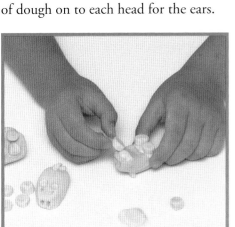

4 When cool, join four legs on to each body with salt dough and a dab of water. Place the pigs back in the oven at the same temperature for two hours.

5 Allow the finished pigs to cool on a rack before smoothing any rough parts with sandpaper. To finish, paint and varnish your Family of Pigs.

Treasure Chest

This treasure chest is a great place to keep small and precious things. It is made of drying modelling material that slowly hardens when left in the air. The skull and crossbones on the front is the traditional sign of a pirate ship.

Handy hint

Roll out the modelling material for the base and sides of the chest to about 5mm (¼in) in thickness. If the material is rolled too thinly, the sides of the chest may collapse.

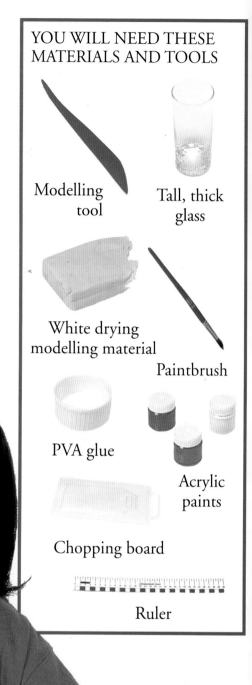

YOU WILL NEED THESE
MATERIALS AND TOOLS

Modelling tool

Tall, thick glass

White drying modelling material

Paintbrush

PVA glue

Acrylic paints

Chopping board

Ruler

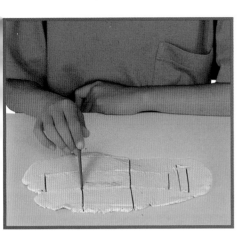

1 Roll out the material. Cut out two sides and a base each 6cm x 4cm (2¹/₂in x 1¹/₂in), and two more sides each 4cm x 4cm (1¹/₂in x 1¹/₂in). Cut a strip 8cm (3in) long for the lid strap.

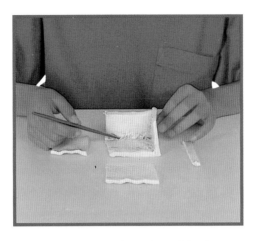

2 Score around the sides of the base with the modelling tool. Position the first side and smooth the inside join. Position the remaining sides and smooth the inside joins.

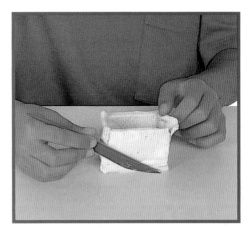

3 When all the sides are in place, smooth the outside edges with the tool. Use the point of the tool to make dots in the modelling material to create the effect of studs.

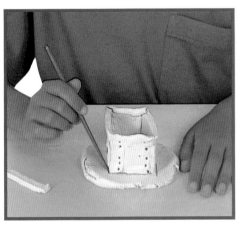

4 Roll out another piece of modelling material and place the chest on it. Cut around the chest so that the rectangle for the lid will be exactly the same size as the base of the chest.

5 Decorate the lid and fix the strap on to the lid. Place the lid on the chest. Decorate the chest with a skull and crossbones cut from modelling material. Allow the chest to dry for 24 hours.

6 When the chest is dry and hard, paint it inside and outside with acrylic paints. Allow the paint to dry before applying a coat of varnish made from 8 parts PVA glue to 1 part water.

The Treasure Chest would make a wonderful birthday or Christmas gift for a friend if filled with chocolate coins wrapped in gold foil. If you want to use your Treasure Chest to store small, fragile valuables, line the treasure chest with cotton wool.

Grinning Cat

This grinning cat looks very pleased with itself. You can almost hear it purring! This model is very simple to make because the cat's legs are curled tightly under its body. Do not make the tail too thin or it will break.

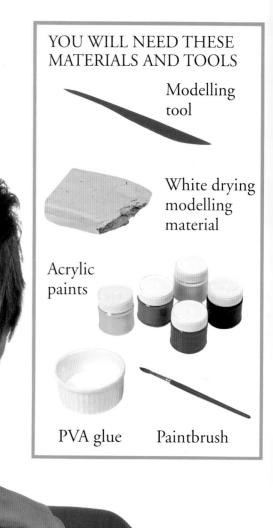

YOU WILL NEED THESE MATERIALS AND TOOLS

Modelling tool

White drying modelling material

Acrylic paints

PVA glue   Paintbrush

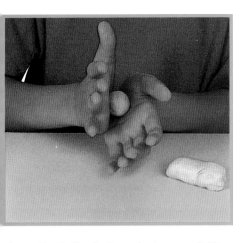

1 Roll a ball of white drying modelling material between your palms to make the head. Then roll a thick sausage 6cm (2¹⁄₂in) long and 2¹⁄₂cm (1in) wide for the cat's sleek body.

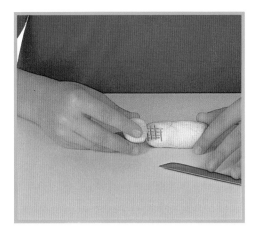

2 To fix the head on to the body, score the bottom of the head with the modelling tool and press the head firmly on to the body. Smooth the join with your fingers.

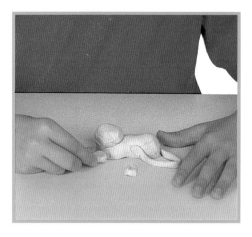

3 Cut and shape two pieces of modelling material to make the front paws. Press them into position. Make a tail and press it on to the body. Curl the tail around the body.

4 Flatten a small piece of modelling material with the palm of the your hand. Use the blade of the modelling tool to cut out two small triangles for the cat's ears.

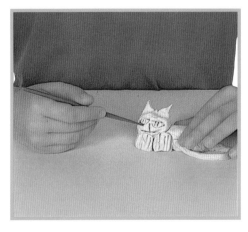

5 Use the modelling tool to carve the features of the cat. You might want to practise this using a piece of leftover material. Allow the cat to dry for about 12 hours before starting to paint it.

6 Carefully paint the cat and use only the very boldest colours. Allow the paint to dry thoroughly before applying a varnish made of 8 parts PVA glue and 1 part water.

Paperweight Cat

Because Grinning Cat does little more all day than sit around looking pleased with itself, it would make a great paperweight. A paperweight stops sheets of paper from being blown around and lost. To make Paperweight Cat, all you have to do is make a larger and therefore heavier model. You will need to allow 24 hours for drying before painting.

Heart and Star Rings

These rings are great fun and easy to make. To make heart and star templates, draw the shapes on to card and cut them out.

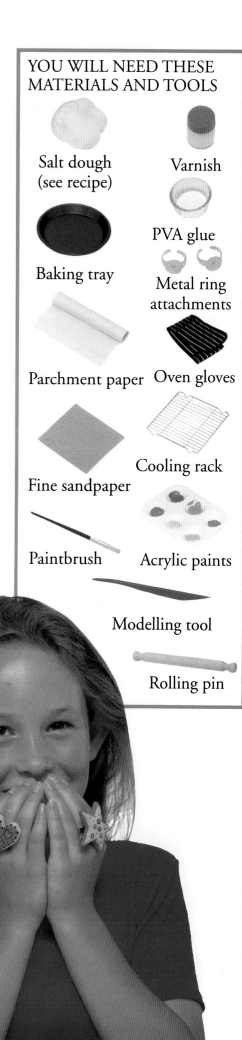

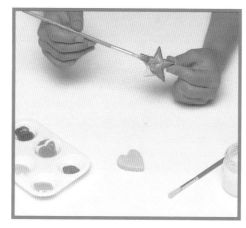

1 Roll out a piece of salt dough 1cm (¹/₂in) thick. Place the heart and star templates on the dough and cut around them. Place the shapes on a baking tray lined with parchment paper and bake them for about four hours at 120°C/250°F/Gas ½.

2 When the shapes have hardened, remove the tray from the oven (using oven gloves) and transfer them to a cooling rack. Once they have cooled, smooth rough edges with sandpaper before painting your rings. When dry, apply a coat of varnish.

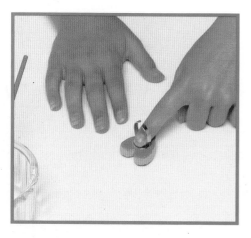

3 Glue a ring attachment on to the back of each shape and leave the glue to dry before trying on the rings.

These rings are so easy to make you will soon be wearing one on each of your fingers!

Heart Throb Bracelet

Dress up for a party and wear this fun bracelet. You could make other bracelets with stars or flowers.

YOU WILL NEED THESE MATERIALS AND TOOLS

Salt dough (see recipe)

Card

Rolling pin

Biscuit cutter

Varnish

Parchment paper

Baking tray

Oven gloves

Cooling rack

Paintbrush

Fine sandpaper

Acrylic paints

Scissors

Glue

1 Roll out a large piece of salt dough to about 1cm (¹/₂in) thick. Using a heart-shaped biscuit cutter, cut out five hearts. Place the hearts on a baking tray lined with parchment paper and bake them in the oven for about four hours at 120°C/250°F/Gas ½.

2 Ask an adult to remove the tray from the oven using oven gloves and to transfer the hardened shapes to the cooling rack. When cool, smooth the edges with sandpaper then paint the hearts in lots of bright colours. When dry, apply a coat of varnish.

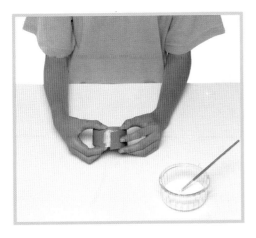

3 Cut a strip of card 20cm x 5cm (8in x 2in). Check that it will fit easily over your wrist before gluing the ends.

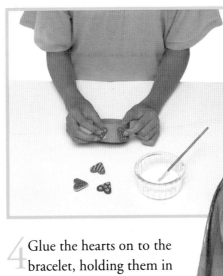

4 Glue the hearts on to the bracelet, holding them in place until the glue sets.

Tyrannosaurus Rex

The Tyrannosaurus Rex is back and it is living in your bedroom! This cheery model of the scariest dinosaur of all has big feet, scaly skin and a winning smile! The Tyrannosaurus Rex is just one type of dinosaur, why not try making the three-horned Triceratops or inventing your own fantastic reptile?

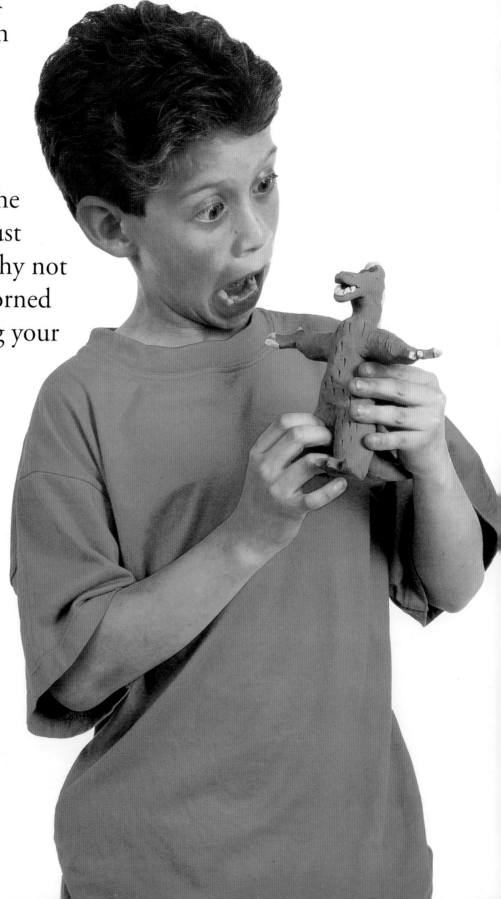

YOU WILL NEED THESE MATERIALS AND TOOLS

Plastic modelling material (green, red, yellow)

Modelling tool

Ruler

Chopping board

1 Roll five sausages 5cm x 2cm (2in x ³/₄in) for the limbs and body. For the head and neck, mould one lump 2cm x 2cm (³/₄in x ³/₄in) and two smaller lumps. For the tail, roll an 8cm (3in) sausage and cut a strip 5cm (3in) long.

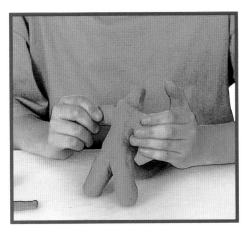

2 Bind the arms, legs, body and tail of the dinosaur together. Use one of the small lumps for a neck. Shape the two remaining lumps into a head. Roll the larger lump into a thick sausage and press the smaller lump on top.

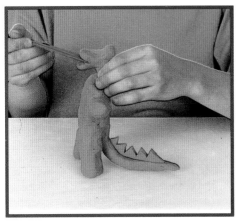

3 Use the tool to carve triangles in the strip of material. Press it on to the tail. Make an opening for the mouth by levering the modelling tool up and down. Take care not to push the dinosaur's head off!

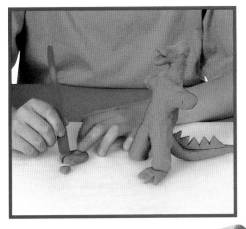

4 Roll out four thick slabs of green material for the feet and hands. Carve the toes and fingers before pressing them into position.

The finishing touch is to texture the surface of your model to create T Rex's scaly reptilian skin. You can do this with the pointy end of your modelling tool or with a cocktail stick.

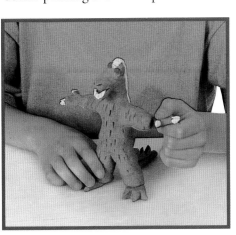

5 Shape red material to make the eyes, and yellow material for teeth, claws and the stripe down the dinosaur's back.

T-shirt
Painting

Petra Boase

Introduction

Decorating T-shirts with fabric paints, glitter and material is fun and very easy to do. In no time at all you will be creating stylish and wacky T-shirts for yourself, friends and family.

T-shirt Painting shows you how to prepare the T-shirts for painting as well as how to use different types of fabric paints to achieve brilliant effects. It is also bursting with ideas. There are T-shirt designs for sports fans, disco dancers, animal lovers and aspiring astronauts. There is even a T-shirt design for bug collectors – this one will give you goosebumps!

Many of these designs can be used for a fancy dress outfit or for school plays. All you need to complete the outfits are leggings or shorts, a hat and a bit of face painting.

Most of the projects are simple to do. A few are more difficult and use special techniques. If you have never done any fabric painting before it might be a good idea to start on one of the easier projects like Swirly Spots, Glitzy Stars, Crazy Spiral or Basketballer.

The colours and types of fabric paints used in the designs are only suggestions. Change them to create different effects and to suit the clothes you will be wearing with the T-shirt. The ultimate design is really up to you. Feel free to modify patterns and to come up with your own ideas.

Disco Dazzler is painted with fluorescent fabric paint that glows under ultra-violet light.

Safety

❖ Always keep fabric paints and sharp utensils out of the reach of small children.

❖ Read the instructions on fabric paint packaging before you start painting. Follow the manufacturer's guidelines for preparing the T-shirt, mixing and applying paints and for drying wet paint. Some manufacturers will also recommend washing or ironing the painted T-shirt before wearing it.

❖ Ask an adult to iron the T-shirt and to supervise the use of sharp tools.

❖ If you splash fabric paint on to your clothes, soak them immediately in lots of cold water. Keep rinsing the garments until the fabric paint is removed. Then wash the clothes in warm, soapy water.

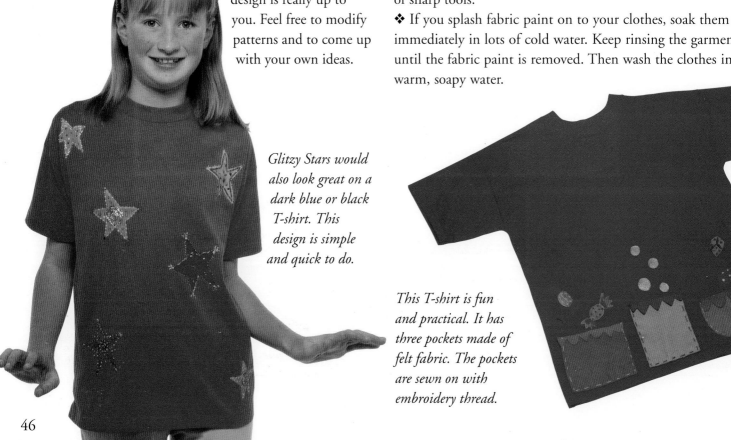

Glitzy Stars would also look great on a dark blue or black T-shirt. This design is simple and quick to do.

This T-shirt is fun and practical. It has three pockets made of felt fabric. The pockets are sewn on with embroidery thread.

Materials and Tools

These are the materials and tools you will need to complete the projects that follow.

Chalk fabric marker This is a special white chalk that is used for drawing outlines on to dark coloured T-shirts.

Fabric glitter This is special glitter that can be fixed to fabric with fabric glue. It is very fine, so use it carefully.

Fabric glue This glue will stick pieces of fabric together. Always use a special brush for applying fabric glue.

Fabric marker pen A fabric marker pen looks like a normal felt-tip pen, but it is designed to be used on fabric.

Fabric paint Fabric paint is applied to fabric and will not wash out. Read the instructions on the container before using it.

Fluorescent fabric paint Under ultra-violet light, this paint will glow. It comes in many bright colours.

Glitter fabric paint This sparkly fabric paint comes in a tube or squeezy container. Always read the instructions on the packaging before using glitter fabric paint.

Hairdryer You will need a hairdryer with a low heat setting to dry puffa fabric paint. Ask permission before using a hairdryer.

Pearl fabric paint This fabric paint dries with a special sheen. It comes in a squeezy container.

Puffa fabric paint When dried with a hairdryer, this paint puffs up. It comes in a squeezy container. Always follow the manufacturer's instructions when using puffa fabric paint.

Sponge You can buy an inexpensive sponge from a chemist shop. A sponge dipped in fabric paint and gently pressed on to fabric makes an interesting texture.

Sticky-back hook and loop dots These dots stick to each other when pressed together.

Stiff card Large pieces of card are inserted into the body and sleeves of a T-shirt to stop wet fabric paint seeping through. You can buy sheets of thick card or use cardboard from recycled packaging and boxes.

T-shirt For the projects you will need cotton T-shirts. There are designs for short and long sleeved styles.

Sponge

Water pot

Puffa fabric paint

Pearl fabric paint

Glitter fabric paint

Stiff card

Embroidery needle

Embroidery thread

Paper

Thick paintbrush

Sewing needle and thread

Ruler

Fabric paints

Medium paintbrush

Tracing paper

Scissors

Fine paintbrush

Newspaper

Fabric marker pen

Sequins

Sticky-back hook and loop dots

Sewing pins

T-shirt

Fluorescent fabric paints

Pencil

Glitter

Fabric glue and brush

Chalk fabric marker

Hairdryer

Ribbons

Felt

Getting Started

Before you can start painting, you must prepare the T-shirt and perfect your design. The more time you spend getting these things right, the more spectacular the results will be.

If you are using a new T-shirt, wash and rinse it to remove excess dye. When the T-shirt is dry, ask an adult to iron it to smooth out creases.

To stop fabric paint seeping through the T-shirt, insert pieces of stiff card into the body and sleeves. The pieces of card should fit snugly into position.

Draw roughs of your design on a piece of paper before drawing it on the T-shirt. Fabric marker pen, like fabric paint, cannot be washed out.

When you are happy with your design, draw it on to the T-shirt. Use a fabric marker pen on light coloured T-shirts. and a chalk marker on dark T-shirts.

When you are ready to start painting and have gathered all the necessary materials and tools, you must cover the work surface with a large sheet of wipe-clean plastic or lots of sheets of newspaper. It is also a good idea to protect any nearby furniture. Fabric paint can splatter, especially if you are flicking a brush loaded with fabric paint to get a special effect. Protect your clothing with an apron and old shirt – fabric paint will not wash off.

Painting tips

Fabric paints come in many wonderful colours and textures, but it is not necessary for you to have everything to create stunning designs on a T-shirt.

Fabric paint colours, just like normal acrylic or poster paint colours, can be mixed together to make other colours. This means, for example, that you can mix blue puffa fabric paint with yellow puffa fabric paint to make green puffa fabric paint. You can also mix glitter fabric paint colours together to make other colours.

To make fabric paint colours lighter, add white fabric paint to the colour or simply add a little water. Fabric paint colours can be made darker by adding a little black fabric paint.

How to mix colours: yellow + blue = green, yellow + red = orange, red + blue = purple.

Mix large quantities of a colour in a water pot or small bowl. Add a little water to paints to make them go further.

Before painting the T-shirt, try out the techniques and the colours on a piece of leftover fabric. This is especially important when using fabric paints in squeezy containers.

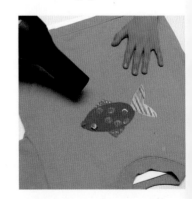

Puffa paint only puffs up when it is dried with a hairdryer, set on low heat. Before drying other fabric paints with a hairdryer, check the instructions on the paint container.

Stencils and Templates

You will need to make stencils and templates to complete some of the T-shirts.

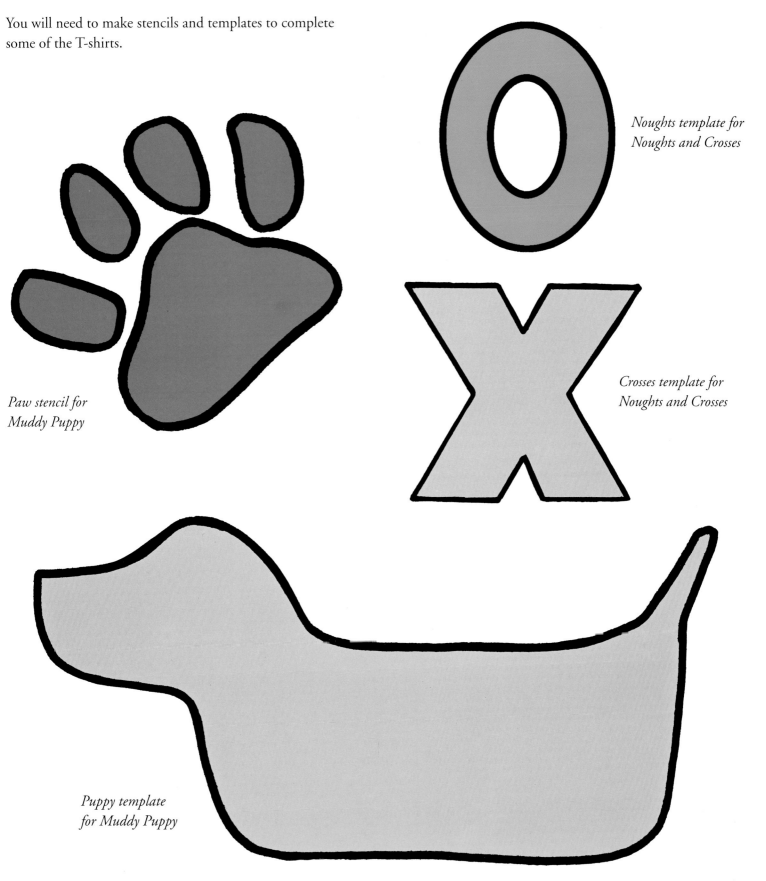

Noughts template for Noughts and Crosses

Crosses template for Noughts and Crosses

Paw stencil for Muddy Puppy

Puppy template for Muddy Puppy

Noughts and Crosses

This T-shirt is great fun. Well, it is not often that an item of clothing doubles up as a board game, is it? Wear it when you are travelling long distances and you will never be bored.

YOU WILL NEED THESE MATERIALS AND TOOLS

2 sheets of card

Short sleeved T-shirt

Ruler

Fabric marker pen

Pencil

Tracing paper

Felt

Scissors

Pearl fabric paint (orange)

10 sticky-back hook and loop dots

Fabric glue and brush

Three noughts in a row means that the boy has won this game of Noughts and Crosses.

1 Insert a piece of card inside the body of the T-shirt. The card should fit snugly. Use a ruler and fabric marker pen to measure and draw the Noughts and Crosses grid. The lines should be 24cm (9½in) long and 8cm (3in) apart.

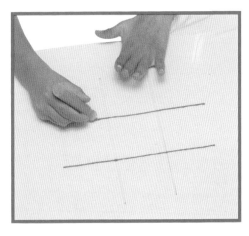

2 Go over the lines with orange pearl fabric paint in a squeezy tube. Move the tube evenly and smoothly along the lines – otherwise the pearl paint will form blobs. Allow the pearl paint to dry thoroughly before continuing.

3 Trace and cut out the nought and cross templates in the Introduction. Place the templates on to the felt and draw around them. You will need five red noughts and five blue crosses. Cut out the shapes. Also cut out five small blue ovals and glue these on to the noughts with fabric glue.

4 Remove the backing from the hoop side of a hook and loop dot. Press the sticky surface on to the back of one of the felt shapes. Repeat for all the remaining shapes.

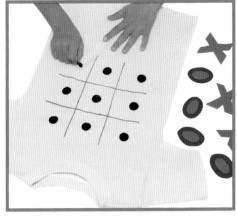

5 Remove the backing from the remaining dots (these will all be looped-sided dots) and press them firmly on to the centre of each square on the grid.

Do not forget to remove the noughts and crosses before washing the T-shirt.

6 You are now ready to play Noughts and Crosses. Have fun!

Sea Life Fantasy

When you look at this T-shirt you can almost smell the salty air, hear the crash of the waves and see the schools of brightly coloured fish darting backward and forward in a pale blue ocean.
In this design there are only two species of marine life, but you could also add crabs, shells, coral and fronds of seaweed.

This T-shirt could also be painted on to a long sleeveless vest or long sleeved sweatshirt. It would also make a wonderfully relaxing image for a pillowcase.

Handy hint

It is good idea to practise your design for this T-shirt on paper before you start drawing it on to the T-shirt. If you have trouble drawing fish or star shapes, trace them from a book or magazine. The underwater world is a fascinating one so if you want to get more ideas for painting your T-shirt, have a look in an encyclopedia or other reference book.

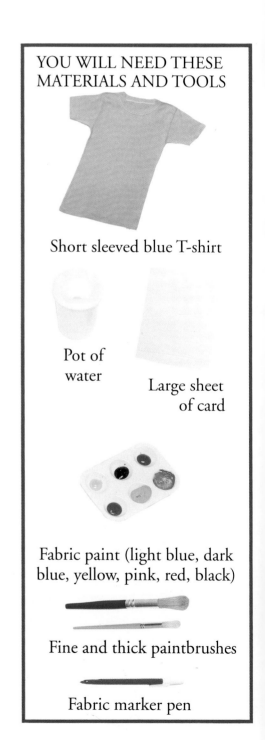

YOU WILL NEED THESE MATERIALS AND TOOLS

Short sleeved blue T-shirt

Pot of water

Large sheet of card

Fabric paint (light blue, dark blue, yellow, pink, red, black)

Fine and thick paintbrushes

Fabric marker pen

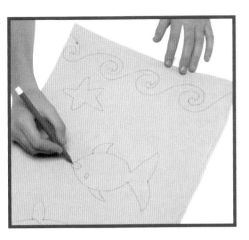

1 Insert the piece of card inside the body of the T-shirt. Use the fabric marker pen to draw the outlines of the fish, starfish and waves on to the front of the T-shirt.

2 Paint the waves with light and dark blue fabric paint using the thick brush. Do not worry if the paint does not go on smoothly – an uneven texture will look more realistic.

3 Paint the fish in shades of blue, green, pink and red. The green can be made by mixing yellow and blue. Use the fine brush to paint the lips and eyes. Paint black bubbles coming from their mouths. Mix red and yellow to make orange. Paint the starfish with the orange paint.

4 Allow the fabric paint to dry. Turn the T-shirt over, making sure that the piece of card is still in position. Use the fabric marker pen to draw another fish on to the back of the T-shirt. Continue the pattern of the waves.

5 Use the thick brush to paint the waves with light and dark blue fabric paint. Wash the brush before painting the fish pink with yellow spots. Paint features on to the fish's face and bubbles coming from its mouth.

Do not forget that this design is called Sea Life Fantasy, so be as creative as you like. You could invent exotic creatures to inhabit a fantastic underwater environment.

Sunny Sunflower

On the Sunny Sunflower T-shirt you can show off your artistic flair for colour, shape and texture. In fact, your painting will be so good that it will be framed in gold. But there is something missing from this painting – the signature of the artist.

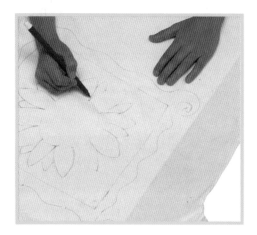

1 Insert a piece of card inside the body of the T-shirt. Use the fabric marker pen to draw the outline of the sunflower and the fancy picture frame.

2 Paint the centre of the sunflower with black fabric paint. Use shades of yellow, red and orange to paint the petals. Allow the paint to dry.

3 Use a sky blue fabric paint for the background of your sunflower painting. Take care not to paint over the petals or into the frame. Allow the paint to dry.

4 Using a clean brush, paint the picture frame with gold fabric paint. For the final artistic touch, decorate the gilt frame with swirls of gold glitter fabric paint.

Optical Illusion

This design is inspired by an artist called Escher. He was famous for his paintings of bizarre optical illusions. In his paintings nothing was ever as it should be – water flowed uphill and darting fish would become birds before your very eyes.

YOU WILL NEED THESE MATERIALS AND TOOLS

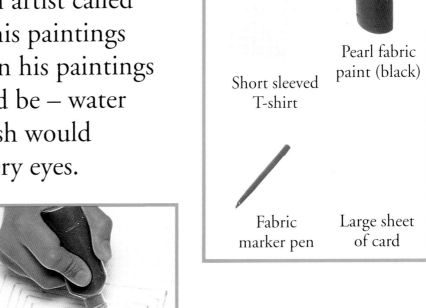

Pearl fabric paint (black)

Short sleeved T-shirt

Fabric marker pen

Large sheet of card

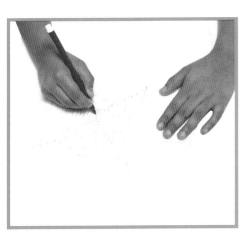

1 Insert a piece of card inside the body of the T-shirt. Use the fabric marker pen to draw a large rectangle on to the front of the T-shirt. Draw more rectangles inside the large rectangle.

2 Go over the design with black pearl fabric paint in a squeezy container. If you are using a new container of pearl fabric paint, cut the nozzle close to the top so that you can paint fine lines.

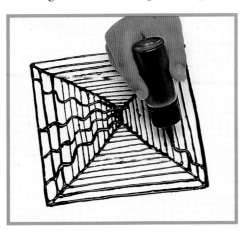

3 Paint lines with black pearl fabric paint from each corner to the middle. Then paint black wiggly lines in the two side triangles, as shown.

To make your Optical Illusion really convincing, divide each line in the bottom triangle into rectangles using the black pearl paint. The rectangles will get smaller as they get closer to the centre. Paint alternate rectangles black to make a checkered pattern.

Bug Collector

Aargh! Do not look now but there are spiders and insects crawling all over you. The Bug Collector T-shirt is not for the squeamish – it is for the enthusiastic mini-beast collector who really wants to bug his friends and family. You can invent your own creatures, or better still, copy them from real life!

This is the perfect T-shirt to wear to a fancy dress party. To make it even more horrifying, stick plastic spiders and other insects on to the T-shirt with double-sided sticky tape. Do not forget to remove your eight- and six-legged plastic friends before you put the T-shirt in to be washed.

Long sleeved T-shirt

Pot of water

Fabric paint (black, red)

Black pearl fabric paint

Large sheet of card

Fine and medium paintbrushes

Fabric marker pen

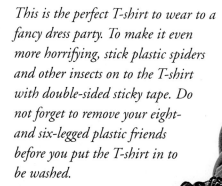

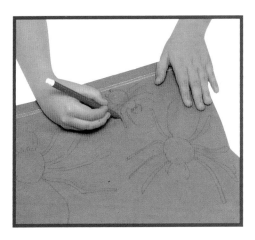

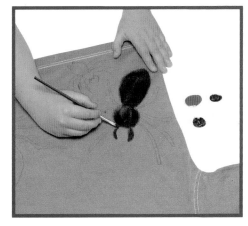

1 Insert pieces of card inside the body and sleeves of the T-shirt. Use the fabric marker pen to draw three very large spiders on to the front of the T-shirt. Draw two or three spiders on to each sleeve.

2 Use the medium brush and black fabric paint to paint the spiders' heads, bodies and fangs. To paint the black jointed legs, use the fine brush. Wash the brush before painting the spiders' eyes red.

3 Dip a finger into black fabric paint and press it on to the T-shirt to make the body and head of a small insect. Repeat until you have covered the front and sleeves of the T-shirt with mini-beasts. Allow to dry.

Potato stamp mini-beasts

To make repeated designs, like small spiders or insects, you can make a stamp with a halved potato. Etch the outline of an insect's body into a cut surface of the potato with a blunt pencil. Ask an adult to cut away the potato from around the shape with a sharp knife. Dip the stamp lightly into fabric paint and press it on to the T-shirt. Keep stamping until you have covered your T-shirt. Paint the legs using black pearl fabric paint. When dry, this paint has a raised and textured finish.

4 To paint legs on the small bugs, use black pearl fabric paint in a squeezy container. Allow the paint to dry thoroughly. If you like, you can paint more spiders and bugs on to the back of the T-shirt.

Swirly Spots

The Swirly Spots design is simple to draw and you can use as many colours as you like. The fabric paint must be dry before you decorate the spots with glitter fabric paint.

Large sheet of card

Short sleeved T-shirt

Medium paintbrush

Fabric marker pen

Pot of water

Fabric paint (red, black, pink, blue, white)

Puffa fabric paint (purple, red, yellow, orange, blue)

Hairdryer

Glitter fabric paint (silver)

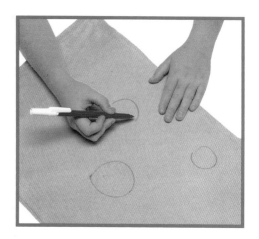

1 Insert pieces of card inside the body and sleeves of the T-shirt. Use the fabric marker pen to draw circles on to the front of the T-shirt. Draw circles on to the sleeves as well.

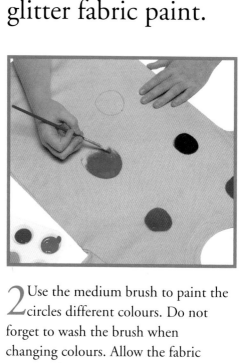

2 Use the medium brush to paint the circles different colours. Do not forget to wash the brush when changing colours. Allow the fabric paint to dry thoroughly before starting the next step.

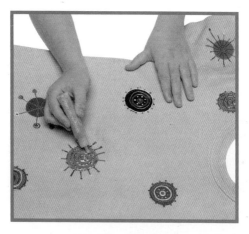

When using fabric paints in squeezy containers, keep the nozzle moving smoothly over your design. If the nozzle stays in one place too long, the paint will form blobs.

3 Use purple, red, yellow, orange and blue puffa fabric paint to decorate the circles with swirls, lines and dots. Dry the puffa fabric paint with the hairdryer. This will make the puffa paint puff up. To finish, decorate some circles with silver glitter fabric paint.

Glitzy Stars

This twinkling T-shirt is perfect for a party. The glitter and sequins will make the stars sparkle under lights. Special fabric glitter can be bought in hobby and craft shops.

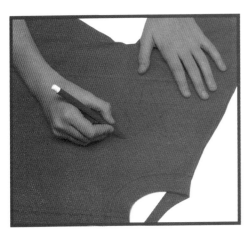

1 Insert a piece of card inside the body of the T-shirt. Use the fabric marker pen to draw the outlines of stars all over the front of the T-shirt. Make some stars large, others small.

2 Use the fine brush to paint the stars with blue, green, red, yellow and pink fabric paints. When dry, paint around the edges of the stars with yellow pearl fabric paint and gold glitter fabric paint. Decorate the stars with dots of yellow and gold.

3 Now it is time to add some real sparkle to this starry T-shirt. Paint the stars with fabric glue. While the glue is still wet, sprinkle on fabric glitter and sequins. When dry, gently shake the T-shirt over a sheet of newspaper to remove excess glitter and sequins.

If you would like to decorate the back of the T-shirt, wait for the front of the T-shirt to dry before turning the T-shirt over. Check that the card is still in place before repeating steps 1, 2 and 3.

59

Disco Dazzler

Wear this wild T-shirt to be the centre of attention. The patterns will positively glow in the dark under ultra-violet light. This is because they have been painted using fluorescent fabric paint.

YOU WILL NEED THESE MATERIALS AND TOOLS

Short sleeved black T-shirt

Pot of water

Hairdryer

Large sheet of card

Chalk fabric marker

Medium paintbrush

Fluorescent fabric paint (yellow, blue, pink, orange, green)

Puffa fabric paint (orange, yellow, purple, red)

1 Insert pieces of card inside the body and sleeves of the T-shirt. Use the chalk fabric marker to draw the outlines of triangles, spirals and zigzag patterns all over the front and the sleeves of the T-shirt. Draw a zigzag pattern along the bottom edge of the T-shirt.

2 Use fluorescent yellow, blue, pink, orange and green fabric paint to fill in the outlines. To make other colours, simply mix different colours together on a palette. Allow the fabric paint to dry before painting patterns on to areas already painted.

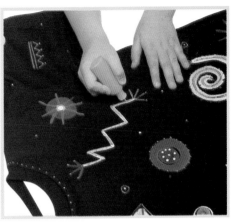

3 Decorate the T-shirt with dots and squiggles of orange, yellow, purple and red puffa fabric paint. You can make your patterns as wild as you like. To make the puffa fabric paint puff up, dry it with a hairdryer. Set the hairdryer to its coolest setting.

4 Go over the zigzag at the bottom of the T-shirt with orange puffa fabric paint. Use other puffa fabric paints to add circles and dots. Once again, use the hairdryer set to its coolest temperature to dry the puffa fabric paint. Allow your T-shirt to dry thoroughly before hitting the disco and dazzling all your friends.

If you want to continue the zigzag pattern on the back of the T-shirt, wait for the front to dry before turning the T-shirt over. Before starting to paint check that the card is still in place.

Dazzling colours

Though this design looks great in fluorescent fabric paint colours, it can also be done using brightly coloured plain fabric paints. Even though these paints will not glow-in-the-dark, your T-shirt will still be the envy of all at the disco. But if you like a bit of glitz and glitter, why not use glitter fabric paint or fabric glitter?

Pockets of Fun

The Pockets of Fun T-shirt means that you will no longer lose or leave at home all your favourite bits and bobs. You can even use one of the pockets for keeping your pocket money safe!

Handy hint

Place a piece of card inside the body of the T-shirt when sewing on the pockets. This will stop you sewing the front and the back of the T-shirt together.

YOU WILL NEED THESE MATERIALS AND TOOLS

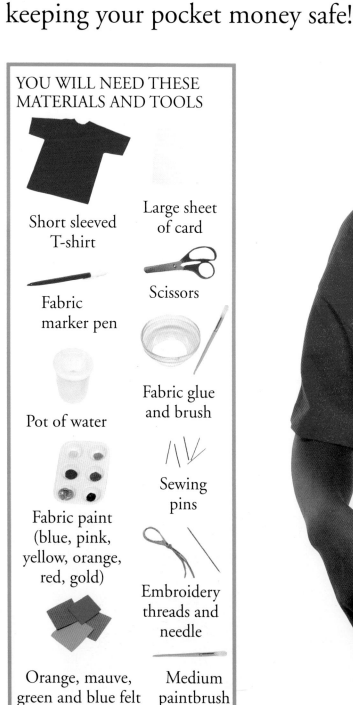

Short sleeved T-shirt

Large sheet of card

Fabric marker pen

Scissors

Pot of water

Fabric glue and brush

Fabric paint (blue, pink, yellow, orange, red, gold)

Sewing pins

Embroidery threads and needle

Orange, mauve, green and blue felt

Medium paintbrush

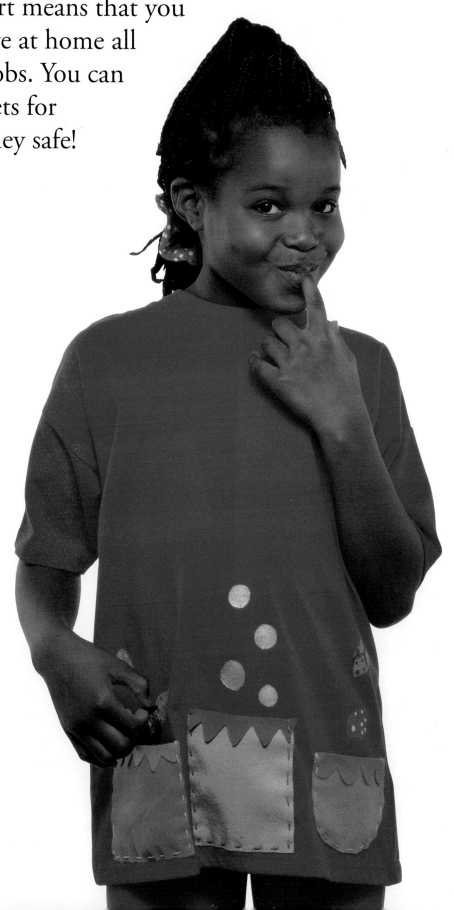

1 Cut three pockets and three decorative strips from the orange, mauve, green and blue felt. The strips must be long enough to fit neatly along the top edge of each pocket. Glue a strip on to the top of each pocket with fabric glue.

2 Position the pockets along the bottom of the T-shirt with pins. Thread the needle with embroidery thread and tie a knot in the end. Use thread that is a different colour from the pocket. Sew the pockets on to the front of the T-shirt using big stitches.

3 Use the fabric marker pen to draw the outlines of sweets, coins and dice just above each pocket. Here are ideas for other items you could draw on your Pockets of Fun T-shirt – pencils, rubbers, jewellery, sunglasses, favourite toys, lipstick and hair clips.

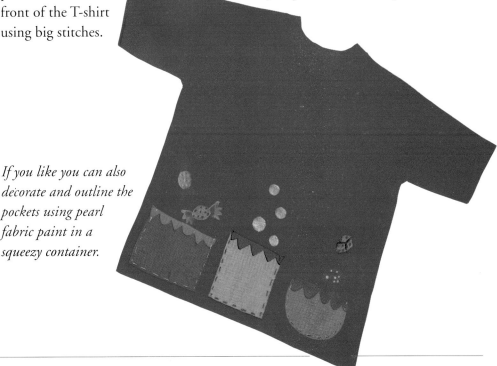

If you like you can also decorate and outline the pockets using pearl fabric paint in a squeezy container.

4 Insert a piece of card into the body of the T-shirt. Paint the dice and sweet wrappers in bright colours. Use gold fabric paint for the coins. Allow fabric paints to dry thoroughly.

Sewing tips

1. To tie a knot, form a loop near end of the thread. Pass the free end of the thread through the loop then pull on the thread.
2. To sew, push the needle up through the fabric and pull till the thread tightens. Move the needle forward then push it down through the fabric. Keep pushing the needle up and down until the pocket is stitched on.

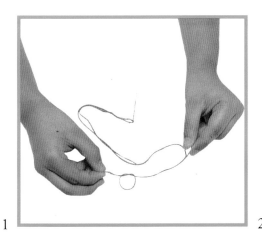

1

2

Basketballer

If you can slam dunk and dribble, then this is the T-shirt design for you. Why not get friends together to form a basketball team? You can have a different number each and choose your own team colours.

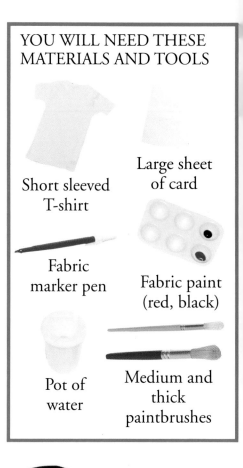

1 Insert card inside the body and sleeves of the T-shirt. Use the fabric marker pen to outline the number 7 on to the front. Draw two bands along the edge of each sleeve front.

2 Use the thick brush to fill in the outline of the number and the bands on each sleeve with red fabric paint. Allow the paint to dry. Use the medium brush to paint a black line around the number and above the red band on the sleeve.

To make your T-shirt look professional, use a ruler when drawing the outlines of the number.

3 Paint the ribbing around the neck of the T-shirt with black fabric paint. When dry, use the medium brush to paint the narrow red line. Allow to dry. Turn over the T-shirt and repeat steps 1, 2 and 3.

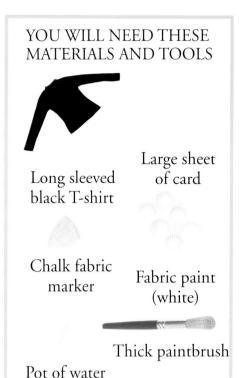

Skeleton

This T-shirt is perfect for a fancy dress party. All you need to complete your nightmare outfit is a black cap, black leggings and a pair of black gloves. Make up your face with white face paint and black eye shadow.

YOU WILL NEED THESE MATERIALS AND TOOLS

Long sleeved black T-shirt

Large sheet of card

Chalk fabric marker

Fabric paint (white)

Thick paintbrush

Pot of water

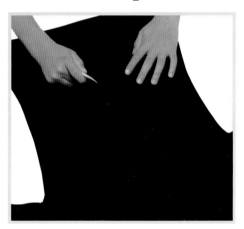

1 Insert card inside the T-shirt body and sleeves. Use the chalk fabric marker to draw outlines of the shoulder blades, rib cage, spine and hips on to the front of the T-shirt. Draw outlines of the arm bones on to both sleeves.

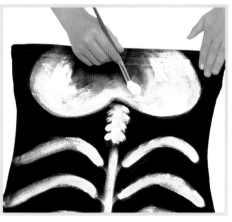

2 Use the thick brush to paint the bones on the front of the T-shirt with white fabric paint. To make the bones really white, do two coats. Allow the paint to dry between coats.

To repeat this design on to the back, allow the T-shirt to dry then turn it over and repeat steps 1, 2 and 3.

3 To finish off, paint the bones on both sleeves. Leave the white fabric paint to dry thoroughly between coats. All you have to do now, Bones the Skeleton, is wait for a full Moon!

Crazy Spiral

The Crazy Spiral T-shirt is simple to do, even if you are new to fabric painting. Draw the outline of the spiral as large as you can to make it easy to paint and to decorate. You can add smaller spirals to the design or paint a spiral on the back of your T-shirt, too.

Handy hint

To stop the T-shirt moving around when you are drawing the outline or painting your design, fix the T-shirt to your work surface with masking tape. Lay the T-shirt out flat, making sure there are no uneven surfaces or bumps, before taping.

YOU WILL NEED THESE MATERIALS AND TOOLS

Short sleeved T-shirt

Large sheet of card

Fabric marker pen

Fine, medium and thick paintbrushes

Glitter fabric paint (green, purple)

Pot of water

Fabric paint (black, orange, yellow, light blue, green)

Pearl fabric paint (yellow, orange, purple)

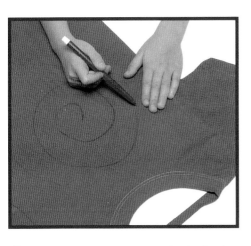

1 Insert pieces of card inside the body and sleeves of the T-shirt. Use the fabric marker pen to draw a large curly spiral on the front of the T-shirt.

2 Paint the spiral with black fabric paint using the thick brush. Allow the paint to dry thoroughly before starting the next step.

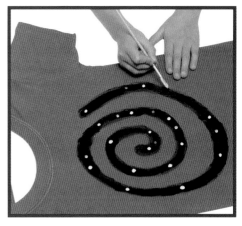

3 Decorate the spiral with orange, yellow, light blue and green dots of fabric paint. Do this using the medium brush. Allow the paint to dry.

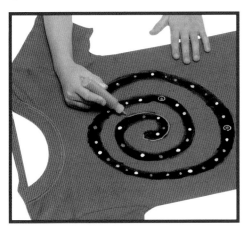

4 Draw circles around some of the dots using yellow pearl fabric paint. Go around the outline of the spiral with orange and purple pearl fabric paint.

5 Make dots of yellow pearl fabric paint inside the spiral. Cover the front of the T-shirt with green glitter fabric paint dots. To finish, dot the sleeves with purple glitter fabric paint.

Choosing your own colours

The colours used on this design are suggestions only – you can choose any combination of colours you like. You could paint the design using only yellows and oranges, or shades of pink and red. Make sure before you start that your colours will stand out against the colour of the T-shirt.

Space Trekker

This T-shirt goes where no other T-shirt has gone before. Its glowing fluorescent yellow after-burners will be seen by alien beings in every far-flung galaxy and planet. But all Space Trekkers should make sure that they know how to get back to Planet Earth!

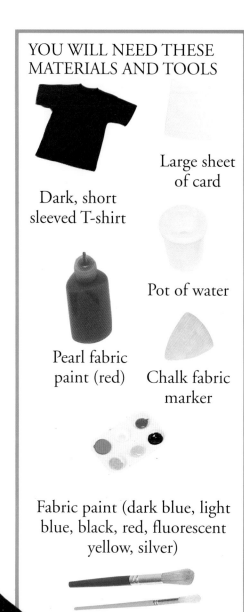

YOU WILL NEED THESE MATERIALS AND TOOLS

Dark, short sleeved T-shirt

Large sheet of card

Pot of water

Pearl fabric paint (red)

Chalk fabric marker

Fabric paint (dark blue, light blue, black, red, fluorescent yellow, silver)

Medium and thick paintbrushes

This Earth-bound Space Trekker dreams of blasting off in his rocket and crashing through the Earth's atmosphere. He wants to discover the secrets of the Solar System and find out about life on other planets.

1 Insert card inside the body and sleeves of the T-shirt. Use the chalk fabric marker to outline the planets, stars and rocket. Draw only the end of the rocket on to the front of the T-shirt.

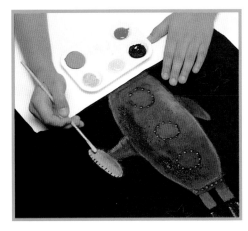

2 Use the medium and thick brushes to paint the rocket with dark blue, light blue, black and red fabric paint. Use fluorescent yellow fabric paint for the rivets and after-burners. Paint the top of the rocket silver.

3 Paint the stars with silver fabric paint. Use plain and fluorescent fabric paints for the planets. When dry, make a ring around each planet with red pearl fabric paint. Use the pearl fabric paint to add details to the rocket.

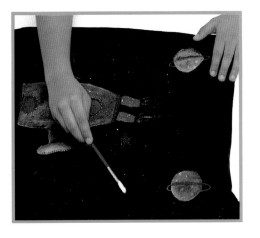

4 To make galaxies of stars, dip the thick brush in yellow fluorescent fabric paint and then flick the brush at the T-shirt. Allow to dry.

5 Turn the T-shirt over. Use the chalk fabric marker to draw the nose of the rocket to line up with the section on the front. Paint the rocket and stars as before.

Paint the Solar System

Imagine how impressed your teacher would be if you painted the Solar System on to your Space Trekker T-shirt. You know that the Earth looks like a green and blue ball from Outer Space, but do you know what the other eight planets look like? To find out about Mercury, Venus, Mars, Jupiter, Saturn, Uranus, Neptune and Pluto, find some pictures in a reference book.

Muddy Puppy

Oh, no! Someone has let the puppy walk all over this T-shirt with its muddy paws! Surely such a naughty puppy does not deserve to be given a big, juicy bone! To stop the puppy covering everything with mud, it has been given a fancy pair of socks to wear.

This boy just cannot believe what the Muddy Puppy has done to his white T-shirt. To find out for yourself, look on the next page.

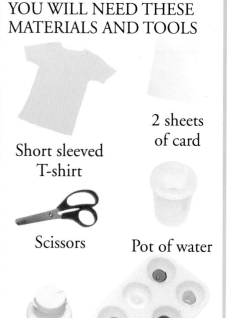

YOU WILL NEED THESE MATERIALS AND TOOLS

Short sleeved T-shirt

2 sheets of card

Scissors

Pot of water

Fabric paint (brown, black, white, turquoise, red, pale blue, yellow)

Fine and thick paintbrushes

Fabric marker pen

Pencil

Fabric glue and brush

Tracing paper

Sponge

Narrow yellow ribbon

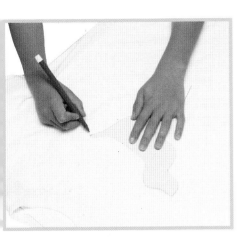

1 Insert card inside the T-shirt body and sleeves. Trace the puppy template in the Introduction. Place the template on to the front of the T-shirt. Draw around it with the fabric marker pen.

2 Paint the dog brown using the thick brush. If you do not have brown paint, make some by mixing together blue, red and yellow. Allow to dry before starting the next step.

3 Use the fine brush to paint black spots on to the body. Continue using the black paint for the ear, tail, shoes and bone. Add features to the face and decorate the socks, shoes and collar.

4 When the paint is dry, tie the ribbon into a small bow. Fix the bow on to the collar with fabric glue. Hold the bow in position until the glue is dry.

5 Trace the paw print stencil in the Introduction. Cut out the stencil, as shown. Turn the T-shirt over, checking that the pieces of card are still in position.

6 Hold the stencil on the T-shirt. Dab the stencil with brown fabric paint. Lift off the stencil. Repeat until the back of the T-shirt is covered with prints.

Stencilling is an easy way to create a repeat pattern. Look through magazines and books to find ideas for other stencils. You could use this same simple technique to cover a T-shirt with cars, flowers, aeroplanes, hearts, stars or even lots and lots of muddy puppies!

Birthday Present

Why not make this T-shirt as a birthday gift for a friend? They could wear it to their own party! It is important that the painted ribbon is identical to the real ribbon. To achieve this, you may have to mix fabric paints together to make the right colour.

As a special treat you could use green, red and gold to paint a Christmas version of the Birthday Present T-shirt. In place of the spotty green ribbon, use a glittery gold ribbon. The dots on the T-shirt could become bunches of holly.

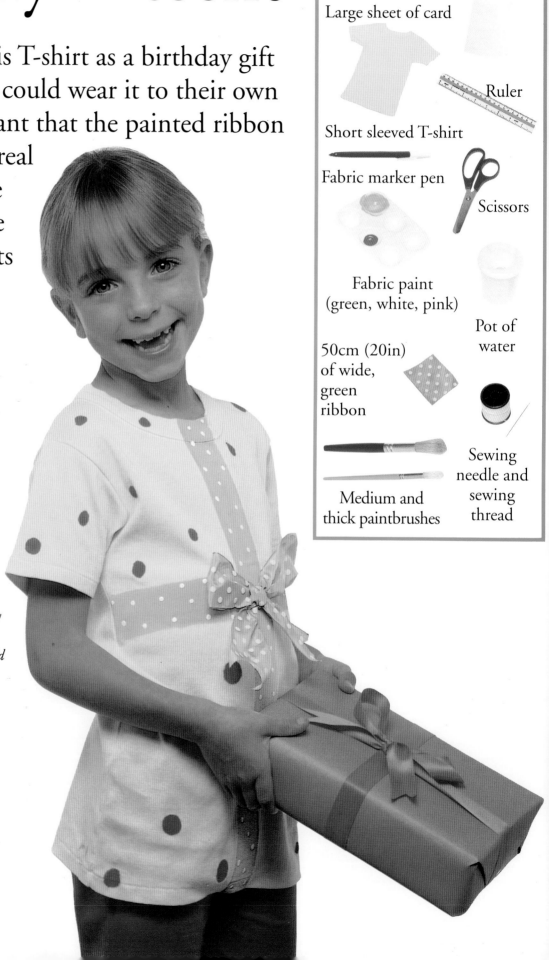

YOU WILL NEED THESE MATERIALS AND TOOLS

Large sheet of card

Ruler

Short sleeved T-shirt

Fabric marker pen

Scissors

Fabric paint (green, white, pink)

Pot of water

50cm (20in) of wide, green ribbon

Sewing needle and sewing thread

Medium and thick paintbrushes

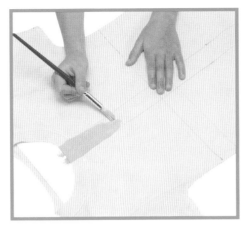

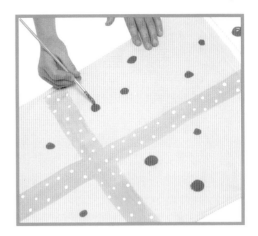

1 Insert pieces of card inside the body and sleeves of the T-shirt. Use the ruler and fabric marker pen to draw two parallel lines down the centre of the T-shirt and two parallel lines across the T-shirt.

2 Paint the area inside the lines with green fabric paint. Do this with the thick brush. These are the pretend ribbons on the present. Make the edges of the ribbon as straight as possible. Allow to dry.

3 Use the medium brush to decorate the painted ribbon with small dots of white fabric paint. Wash and dry the brush before changing fabric paint colours. Cover the rest of the T-shirt with larger pink dots. Allow to dry.

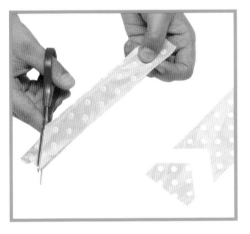

4 Cut a V-shape from both ends of the ribbon to give a neat finish to the birthday present bow.

Making fabric paint go further

When you are painting large areas with fabric paint, it is a good idea to add a little water to the fabric paint. This will make your fabric paints last longer and make them easier to apply. It will also make the colour slightly lighter and may take longer to dry. The more water you add, the lighter the colour will become. Do not make the fabric paint too runny or it will drip all over the place.

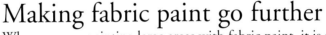

5 Tie the ribbon into a bow. Thread the needle and tie a knot in the end. Position the bow where the painted ribbons cross and sew it into place.

Friendship Bracelets

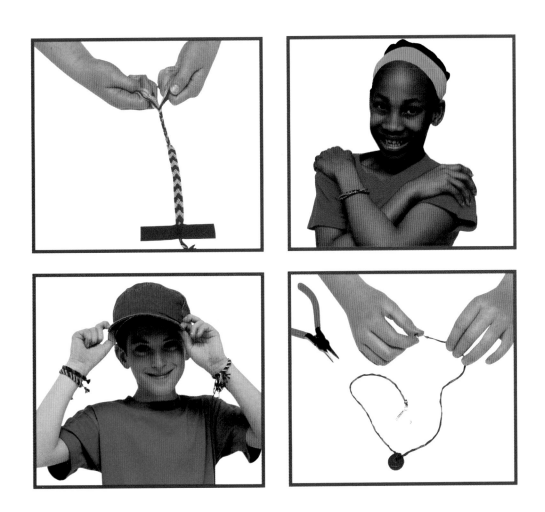

Petra Boase

Introduction

Friendship bracelets are a symbol of friendship, which is why they make such fun presents for your friends and family. You could make matching friendship bracelets for you and your best pal, or weave a bracelet, anklet or necklace using the colours of your favourite sports team. But there is one more good thing about friendship bracelets – anyone can wear them – teenagers, young children and even adults!

Make them anywhere

Braiding and weaving friendship bracelets can be done anywhere – outside in the garden, on holidays, at the kitchen table or at friends' houses. You do not need to carry around big bags of equipment – all you need are threads, tape, scissors, beads and a smooth work surface. This means that friendship bracelets are also very inexpensive to make.

It is a good idea to store your braiding materials in a bag or small box. This will keep everything clean and ready for when you want to have a bit of fun.

This Hippy Headband is made using the same braiding techniques that are used to make friendship bracelets.

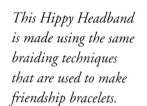

Practice makes perfect

Some of the bracelet designs we show you are quite complicated. They may use many threads, and the knotting and braiding techniques may be a little fiddly. But there are also many designs that even novice braiders will be able to perfect first time.

If you are having trouble making a particular bracelet, do not give up – try again after reading the instructions through and looking closely at the photographs. Your patience will be rewarded when you wear your own hand-made bracelet and all your friends want to know where you bought it!

Experiment with colours

Once you have the knack of braiding and beading, let your imagination run wild and design your very own range of jewellery and accessories. You will soon be experimenting with your own combinations of colours and adding beads and decorations to your bracelets. You will also discover lots of new and exciting threads that will add unusual textures to your designs.

It is very easy to knot colourful beads into friendship bracelets and necklaces.

Materials

These are the materials and tools you will need to complete the following projects.

Beads These come in a wide variety of different sizes, colours, textures and patterns. Tiny or small beads usually have very small holes, so it is easier to thread them on to fine sewing thread, or to sew them on to items using needle and thread. Medium and large size beads are perfect for using with thicker yarns. Metallic beads are shiny and add an extra sparkle to your handiwork.

Cotton knitting yarn This type of yarn is very chunky. Use cotton knitting yarn when you want to make a thick bracelet or anklet. It is available in many bright colours.

Electrical tape This is a strong sticky tape. It is very good for fastening threads to a work surface. You can buy it from electrical and hardware shops.

Hair clip This hair accessory has a metal clip that grips the hair. The top of the hair clip is made of plastic.

Jewellery clamp A jewellery clamp can be fastened over the knot at each end of a friendship cord to finish it off. Jewellery fasteners can be attached to clamps.

Jewellery fastener This is a releasable metal clasp that can be used to secure a bracelet or necklace.

Metal rings These small metal loops are used to attach jewellery fasteners to jewellery clamps.

Pliers Use small jewellery pliers or fine-nosed pliers to open and close metal rings and to secure jewellery clamps. Many types of pliers have a cutting edge, so always ask for adult help when you use pliers.

Soft embroidery thread This is a thick thread that is ideal for friendship bracelets. It comes in many vibrant colours.

Stranded embroidery thread As its name suggests, this cotton thread is made up of many strands. It is very good for making patterned and knotted friendship bracelets.

Sunglasses attachments These rubber loops are used to attach sunglasses to a strap. Buy them from specialist bead shops.

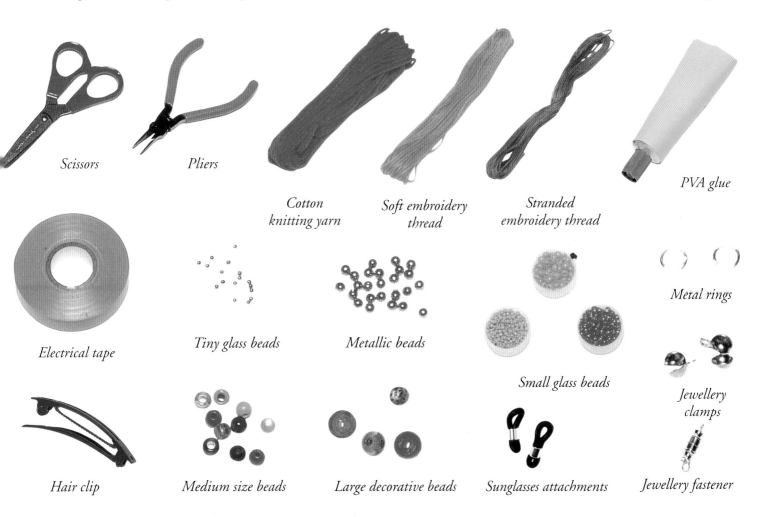

Scissors

Pliers

Cotton knitting yarn

Soft embroidery thread

Stranded embroidery thread

PVA glue

Electrical tape

Tiny glass beads

Metallic beads

Small glass beads

Metal rings

Jewellery clamps

Hair clip

Medium size beads

Large decorative beads

Sunglasses attachments

Jewellery fastener

Basic Techniques

Starting off

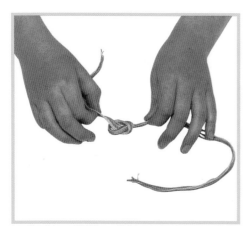

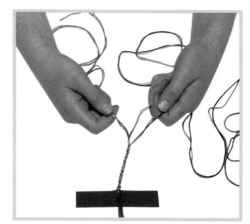

1 Cut the threads to the required length. Check that you are using the right type of thread and have the correct number of threads in each colour. Gather the threads and line up the ends. Tie the threads together with a knot near one end. Each project will tell you exactly where to tie the knot.

2 Secure the threads to your work surface using a piece of electrical tape just above the knot. Press the tape firmly over the threads so that the threads do not come lose. A breadboard, laminated tray or piece of stiff card make excellent portable surfaces on which to do your braiding.

3 Some projects will then ask you to plait a 5cm (2in) length before you start braiding. Try to keep an even pressure on the threads when plaiting so that it remains straight. Secure the end of the plaited section to your work surface with electrical tape. Press the tape firmly over the plait.

Finishing off

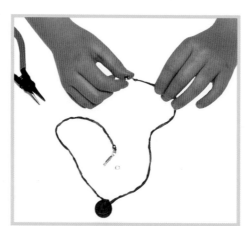

To finish a bracelet - divide the threads at the end of the braid into three even groups and plait together. This plait should be the same length as the one at the other end of the bracelet. Tie a knot at the end of the plait before threading on beads. Keep the beads in place with another tight knot. Trim the threads.

To finish a necklace - tie a tight knot at the end of the braid. Use pliers to close a jewellery clamp over the knots at both ends of the braid. Open the metal rings using pliers and attach a metal ring to each clamp. Separate the sections of the jewellery fastener and attach one section to each ring. Close the rings.

To finish a headband - tie a tight knot close to the end of the braid and thread beads on. You can thread beads on to each thread or use a large bead through which all the threads will pass. To hold the beads in place, tie another knot. The knot must be large enough to stop the bead falling off.

Tying off

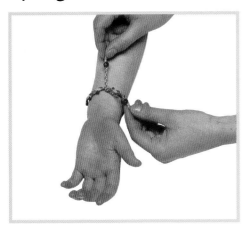

Tying on a bracelet - ask a friend to help tie a double knot. If there is no one around to help, you could tie the bracelet around your ankle instead.

Fastening a necklace - place the necklace around your neck with the opened fasteners at the front. To line up the clasps, look in a mirror.

Tying on a headband - if you cannot do it yourself, ask a friend to tie the ends in a double knot or in a bow at the back of your head.

Braiding tips

The first thing you must do before starting a friendship bracelet design is to carefully read through the instructions and look at the photographs. The second thing to do is make sure you have the right thread and have carefully measured out the lengths needed. Double-check that you have the right number of threads in the right colours.

If you are doing a complicated design it can help to use the same coloured threads as used in the project. Then, when you have mastered that braiding technique, you can go on to make the bracelet, necklace or anklet using your own wonderful colour combinations.

To give your bracelets the professional look, try to keep the tension on the threads even. An uneven tension will make the bracelet twist and buckle.

Using your imagination

The colours and beading ideas used in these projects are just to get you started. There is really no end to the sorts of things you can do to make your friendship bracelets totally unique. Here are some ideas that you might like to try.

❖ Tightly knot together leftover lengths of thread and trim excess threads. When you braid with these multi-coloured threads you will create a bracelet of many colours. These lengths of thread are also useful when trying out a new braiding technique.

❖ Beads with very small holes, buttons and sequins can be sewn on to a completed bracelet using ordinary sewing needle and sewing thread.

❖ Use textured or glittery threads in your designs.

Looking after your materials

❖ To keep your leftover threads in order, wind them around rectangles of thick card. To stop them unravelling, insert the thread ends into a small slot cut into one edge of the card.

❖ To keep your scissors sharp, do not use them to cut paper.

❖ Store your beads and jewellery equipment in lidded containers. This will stop you losing them and, more importantly, will keep them out of reach of young children.

Twisty Bracelet

This bracelet is almost like mixing a palette of coloured paints. But instead of using paints, you are twisting threads together to make new colours.

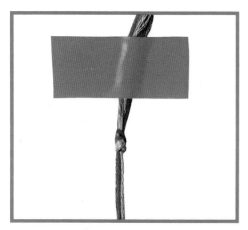

1 You will need six threads of different colours, each 70cm (27in) long. Tie them in a knot, 10cm (4in) from the top of the threads. Fasten them on to your work surface with electrical tape just above the knot.

2 Hold the ends of the threads together and twist them together in the same direction until they feel tight. The threads will start to get shorter.

3 Pull the twisted length straight and place your finger in the centre of it. Fold the twisted length in half and carefully remove your finger. As you do this, the twisted threads will wind around each other.

Handy hint

Be sure to hold on tightly to the twisted braid. If you let go before you have secured it with a knot, the twist will unwind.

4 Remove the electrical tape and tie a knot in the free end. Tie this knot as close to the end as possible. Trim any uneven threads with scissors. To fasten the bracelet around your wrist or ankle, push the knot through the loop at the other end.

Hippy Headband

Dress up as a happy hippy and wear this colourful band around your head. The more threads you use, the wider the plait will be. Why not make a bracelet to match?

YOU WILL NEED THESE MATERIALS

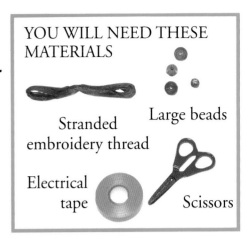

Stranded embroidery thread

Large beads

Electrical tape

Scissors

1 Cut 12 lengths of thread, each 150cm (60in) long. Tie them in a knot 15cm (6in) from the top of the threads and fasten them on to your work surface with a piece of tape just above the knot.

2 Divide the threads into three groups, each with four threads. Continue plaiting the threads until the band is long enough to fit around your head. Try to keep the tension on the threads even or the plait will twist.

3 Tie the threads at the end of the plait in a knot. Remove the tape.

To make it easy to thread the beads on to your headband, wrap a little tape around the end of the threads. This will keep the threads together and stop them from fraying.

4 Thread beads on to both ends of the headband and secure with knots. Thread another bead on to each end and tie another knot. Trim any uneven threads. To make a bracelet to match, cut 12 threads, each 40cm (16in) long. Then follow steps 1 to 4.

Jungle Bracelet

This bracelet is inspired by the colours you would see on an African safari. So when choosing your threads, look out for brown, ochre and yellow. You could choose your own theme, such as a rainbow, a sunset or a season, and select colours to co-ordinate with that theme.

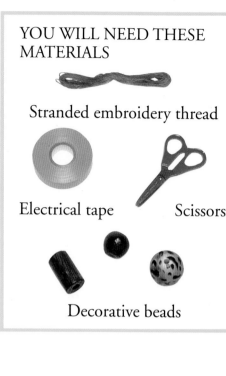

YOU WILL NEED THESE MATERIALS

Stranded embroidery thread

Electrical tape

Scissors

Decorative beads

82

1 Cut three threads of one colour and two of another, each 100cm (40in) long. Tie the threads in a knot, 15cm (6in) from the top. Fasten the threads to the work surface with tape just above the knot. Lay out the threads, as shown.

2 Start with the thread on the far left (in this project it is a brown thread). Take this thread over the orange thread on the right, back under the orange thread, through the loop and over itself. Pull gently to make a knot and repeat.

3 Continue the same knotting technique as shown in step 2, making two knots on each of the remaining threads on the right, until you get to the end of the first row. The brown thread will finish on the right.

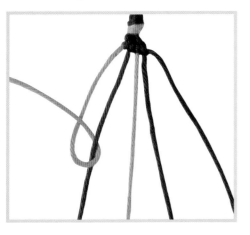

4 Take the new thread on the far left (an orange thread) and make a new row of knots as shown in steps 2 and 3.

5 Continue knotting the bracelet until it is the right length to fit around your wrist or ankle. Tie the threads in a knot to secure the braid.

Easy way to learn

If you have never made friendship bracelets before it may help if you use the same colour threads as used in the photographs. This will make it much easier for you to follow the steps and use the correct threads. When you have mastered a braiding technique, then you can go on to create one using your favourite colours.

6 Plait the loose threads for 5cm (2in) and tie the end of the plait in a knot. Thread a bead on to each thread. Secure each bead with a knot.

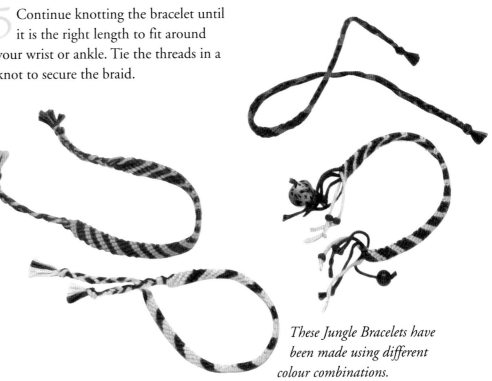

These Jungle Bracelets have been made using different colour combinations.

Woven Bracelet

This popular style of friendship bracelet uses a very easy weaving technique. If you want to make a really wide bracelet, weave two bracelets and then sew them together using embroidery thread and needle.

YOU WILL NEED THESE MATERIALS

Cotton knitting yarn

Electrical tape

Scissors

Woven Bracelets look really good in strong, bold colours like red and yellow, purple and blue or even black and white. When weaving this bracelet, hold the threads tightly, otherwise the threads will unwind and you will have to start all over again!

1 Cut two threads in one colour and two in another, each 80cm (31in) long. Fold them in half and tie the ends by the fold in a knot, 5cm (2in) from the top. Fasten the threads to your work surface with tape close to the knot. Arrange the threads in colour pairs.

2 Start with the far right pair of threads (in this project they are blue) and take them under the blue pair and purple pair next to them, then back over the purple pair. Leave them in the middle, as shown.

3 Take the pair of purple threads on the far left that you have not used yet. Take these threads under the purple and blue pairs next to them, then back over the blue pair. Leave the purple pair in the middle.

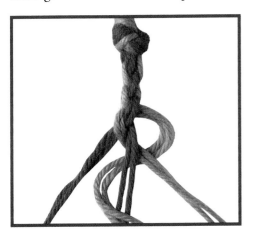

Woven belt

If you have lots of patience and reams of chunky cotton yard or knitting wool you can make a woven belt. Take your waist measurement and cut lengths of yarn that are three times the size of your waist measurement. If you want long lengths of loose threads at the ends, cut them a little longer. Make your woven belt following the instructions for Woven Bracelet.

4 Pull the pairs of threads up tightly to the top. Then go back to the blue pair of threads on the far right and repeat steps 2 and 3 until the bracelet is long enough to fit around your wrist.

5 Tie the threads in a knot at the end of the weaving. Snip the looped threads at the top of the braid. You can leave the ends as they are or plait them.

Funky Bracelet

This chunky bracelet uses ten strands of knitting yarn. You have to hold the threads firmly, or the weaving will be uneven.

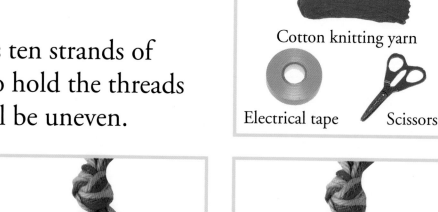

1 Cut five different coloured threads, each 80cm (32in) long. Fold the threads in half and tie in a knot, 5cm (2in) from the fold. Fasten the threads to your work surface with tape above the knot. Lay the threads out as shown.

2 Start with the far right pair of threads (in this project they are yellow) and weave them over the pink pair, under the blue pair, over the green pair and under the purple pair. Pull the yellow threads up tightly and leave on the left.

3 Take the pink pair and weave them over the blue pair, under the green pair, over the purple pair and under the yellow pair. Pull the pink threads up tightly and leave on the left.

To make a Funky Bracelet or anklet for a special occasion, you could replace two coloured threads with glittery gold and silver threads.

4 Repeat steps 2 and 3 with each new pair of threads on the far right, until the braid is the right length. Tie the end in a knot and cut the top loop.

Hair Wrap

These braids look great! Take it in turns with a friend to do each other's hair. Finish off the braid with two beads tied on to the end.

YOU WILL NEED THESE MATERIALS

Cotton knitting yarn

Scissors

Medium size beads

1 Cut three lengths of different coloured thread, twice the length of the hair you are braiding. Take a 1cm (¹/₂in) section of hair and knot the centre of the threads around the hair, close to the scalp.

2 Hold the section of hair away from the head. Select one of the coloured threads and start winding it tightly around the hair and the other threads. The loops of thread should lie very close together.

3 When you have wound as much as you want of the first colour, start winding a thread of another colour in the same way. Keep alternating the colours until you reach the end of the hair.

4 To finish off, thread a few beads on to the end of the hair and tie a knot in the thread to stop the beads falling off. Knot the threads around the hair to stop the wrap unravelling. When you want to remove the wrap, cut off the knot and beads at the end of the wrap and unwind the threads.

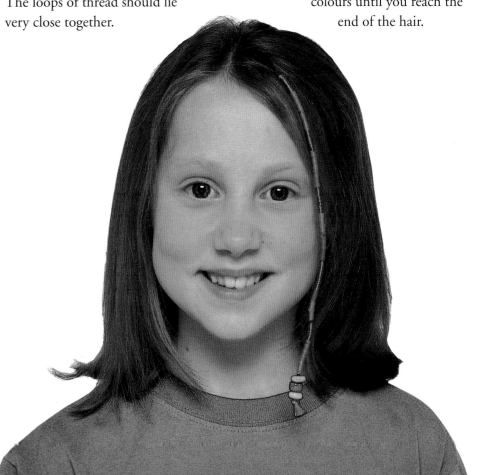

Stripes Galore Bracelet

This is one of the most popular styles of friendship bracelet and, if you are a beginner, it is a good one to start with. The more threads you have, the wider the bracelet will be. The more colours you use, the brighter it will be.

Handy hint

This bracelet consists of wide stripes in three colours, but you can also braid it using six threads of different colours. The stripes will be narrower, but your bracelet will be much more colourful. To make this really stripy bracelet, choose six threads of contrasting colours and follow the instructions in steps 1 to 6.

YOU WILL NEED THESE MATERIALS

Stranded embroidery thread

Electrical tape   Scissors

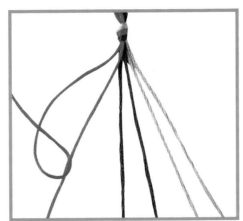

1 Cut six threads, two of each colour and each 100cm (40in) long. Knot them together, 10cm (4in) from the top of the threads. Fasten the threads to your work surface with tape, close to the knot. Lay the threads out as shown.

2 Start with the thread on the far left (in this project it is a pink thread). Take the thread over the pink thread next to it, then back under the pink thread, through the loop and over itself. Pull the thread gently to make a knot.

3 Repeat step 2. Still using the same thread, make two knots on the purple thread. Continue to knot the remaining purple and green threads with the pink thread in the same way until you reach the end of the first row.

4 Go back to the new thread on the far left, which is another pink thread, and repeat steps 2 and 3 to make another row. Now the new thread on the far left will be a purple thread. Knot it in the same way

5 Continue knotting each new far left thread over the other threads to build up stripes of the three different colours. Keep braiding until the bracelet is the right length to fit around your wrist or ankle.

6 Tie the threads at the end of the braid in a knot. Plait the loose threads at both ends of the bracelet for 6cm (2¹/₂in) and secure the plaits with knots. Carefully trim any uneven threads with scissors.

The Stripes Galore Bracelet on the right has been finished with plaits. The bracelet on the left has not been plaited, therefore leaving long, loose threads.

Stripes and Beads Bracelet

This bracelet has beads threaded into it to add extra sparkle, colour and texture. Use small or medium size beads, but make sure the hole of each bead is large enough for the thread to fit through.

Handy hint

It is a good idea to sort out which beads you are going to use before you start braiding the bracelet. It is hard enough keeping hold of the right threads without having to fumble around in a jar of beads at the same time.

YOU WILL NEED THESE MATERIALS

Soft embroidery thread

Electrical tape

Scissors

Small and medium beads

1 You will need four threads 100cm (40in) long. Tie the threads in a knot, 10cm (4in) from one end. Fasten them to the work surface with tape above the knot. Lay threads as shown.

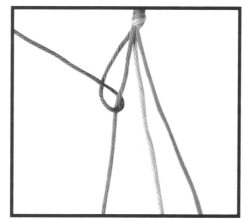

2 Take the thread on the left (a purple thread) over the pink thread next to it and back under, through the loop and over itself. Pull the thread to make a knot. Repeat to make another knot.

3 Make the same knots on the blue and the orange threads using the purple thread. You will now have finished the first row and the purple thread should be on the right.

4 Go back to the new thread on the left (a pink thread) and thread a bead on to it. Knot the pink thread following steps 2 and 3.

5 Go back to the new colour on the left (a blue thread). Knot this thread over the first two threads (orange and purple) and, before you knot it over the pink, thread a bead on to the pink thread and then knot the blue thread over it. This knot will secure the bead.

Fraying threads

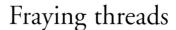

The ends of the threads become quite ragged when threaded through beads. To prevent this, wrap a small piece of sticky tape around the ends of each thread before you start braiding.

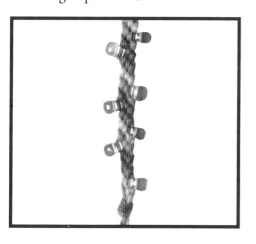

6 Continue to knot and thread on beads until the bracelet is the right length. Tie the threads in a knot.

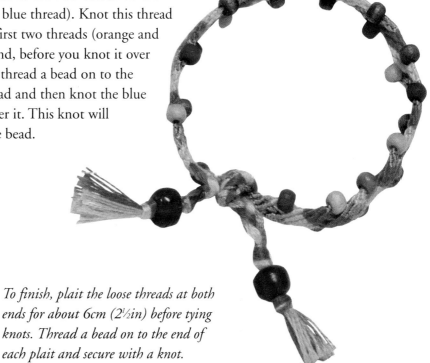

To finish, plait the loose threads at both ends for about 6cm (2½in) before tying knots. Thread a bead on to the end of each plait and secure with a knot.

Noughts and Crosses

The Noughts and Crosses bracelet will really impress your friends! It looks terrific in black and white, but could also be braided using the colours of your favourite football team.

1 You will need eight pieces of thread in two colours, each 100cm (40in) long. Tie the threads in a knot and plait them for 5cm (2in). Fasten the threads to the work surface with tape at the end of the plait. Lay out threads as shown.

2 Take the thread on the far left (in this project it is purple) and tie two knots on each of the three threads to its right. Leave the purple thread in the middle. Repeat with the purple thread on the far right.

3 Take the purple thread on the middle right and knot it over the middle left thread. Do two knots. Repeat steps 2 and 3 using the three outer pairs of threads. Start with the outermost thread on the left.

4 Knot the far right purple thread over the purple thread next to it. Do two knots. Repeat with far left purple thread.

5 Using the fourth thread from the left, do three knots on each of the threads to its left. Repeat with fourth thread from right.

6 Knot the new middle right thread over the middle left thread, twice. Repeat step 5 to make a cross. Repeat steps 5 and 6 using the purple threads. Knot the middle left pink thread over the thread to its left, twice.

Contrasting thread colours, like green and yellow or yellow and purple, makes the Noughts and Crosses design stand out.

7 Knot the middle right pink thread over the thread to its left, twice. Next, knot the middle right thread over the middle left thread, twice.

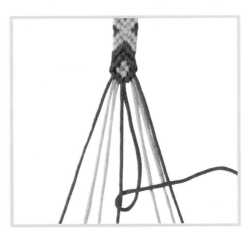

8 To complete the design, repeat from step 2 onwards until your bracelet is the right length. To finish, plait 5cm (2in) and tie a knot and trim the ends.

Stripy Beaded Hair Clip

Handy hint

To put dangling beads on to the other end of your braid, carefully undo the knot at the top of the braid. Trim the threads to the same length as those on the other end and then follow the instructions in step 5. Glue the braid to the top of the hair clip, making sure that the braid is centred on the hair clip.

This hair clip really stands out and it is useful, too. It looks great with any hairstyle or length of hair.

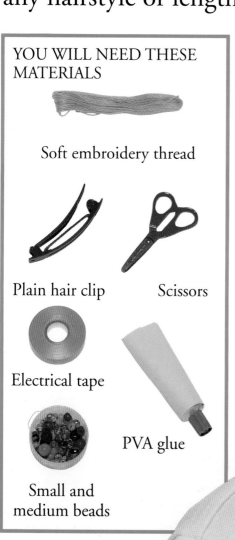

YOU WILL NEED THESE MATERIALS

Soft embroidery thread

Plain hair clip

Scissors

Electrical tape

PVA glue

Small and medium beads

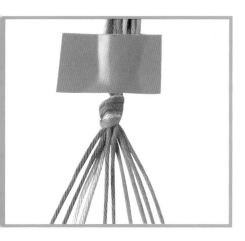

1 Cut ten lengths of thread, two of each colour and each 80cm (32in) long. Tie the threads in a knot, 15cm (6in) from the top. Tape threads to the work surface. Lay threads, as shown.

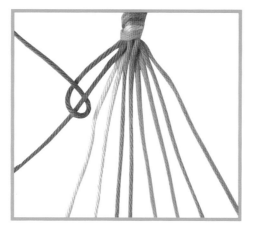

2 Take the dark blue thread on the left over the pale blue thread next to it, back under the thread, through the loop and over itself. Pull the thread gently and repeat the knot.

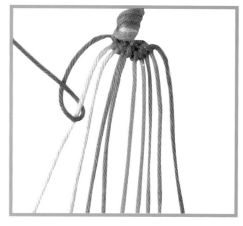

3 Do the same knots on the other threads in the row until the thread you started with is at the end of the row. Go back to the new thread on the far left (another dark blue thread) and repeat the knotting technique explained in steps 2 and 3.

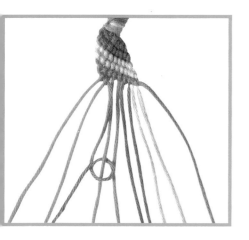

4 Continue knotting the rows with each new far left thread, building up stripes of different colours, until the braid is the same length as the hair clip.

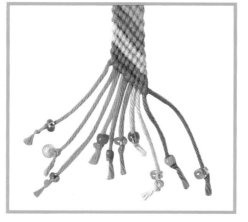

5 Thread small beads on to the end of each thread. Tie a knot on each thread to stop the beads falling off.

6 Apply glue to the back of the braid and stick it to the top of the clip. Fold the knotted end of the braid to the underside of the clip and glue.

Knotty Dotty Necklace

Choose lots of your favourite beads to knot into this colourful necklace, or select one really beautiful big bead to knot halfway along the necklace. If you do not have a jewellery fastener to secure your necklace around your neck, tie the ends in a knot.

Handy hint

Before you start braiding, check that the holes in the beads are large enough for the thread to pass through. Craft and hobby shops sell beads made specially for braiding.

YOU WILL NEED THESE MATERIALS

Stranded embroidery thread

Pliers

Scissors

Electrical tape

Jewellery fastener

2 metal rings

2 jewellery clamps

Small and medium beads

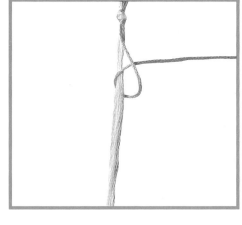

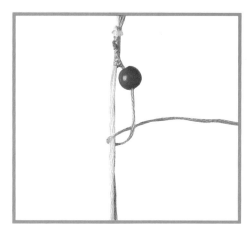

1 Cut four threads, two of each colour and each 150cm (60in) long. Knot the threads 10cm (4in) from the top. Tape them to the work surface above the knot. Lay the threads, as shown.

2 Start with the thread that is out on its own (a blue thread). Take it over the other threads, then under them and through the loop. Pull this thread up tightly while holding the other threads.

3 After you have knotted a row of about five knots, thread a bead on to the blue thread and then continue to make a few more knots. It is now time to start working with a new thread.

Long necklace

You can also make a longer version of the Knotty Dotty Necklace by simply doubling or even tripling the length of the yarns. Do not forget that you will also need lots more beads to decorate your necklace.

4 Make a new row of knots with the new thread. After five knots, thread on a bead.

5 Continue making rows of knots and adding beads in this way until the necklace is the length you want. Tie all the threads together in a knot.

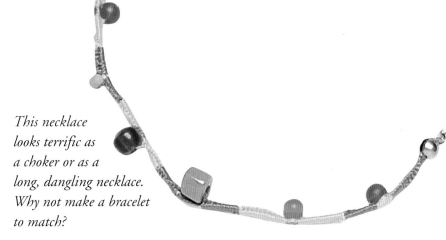

6 Trim the threads close to the knot at each end. Attach a jewellery clamp over each knot and a metal ring to each clamp. Then attach half the jewellery fastener to each of the metal rings.

This necklace looks terrific as a choker or as a long, dangling necklace. Why not make a bracelet to match?

Sunglasses Strap

This Sunglasses Strap is very useful and great fun to wear. When you do not want to wear your sunglasses, you can hang them around your neck. You could make Sunglasses Straps for all the members of your family or as gifts for friends.

Handy hint

Some types of jewellery clamps and rings are made of very tough metal. It may be necessary to ask an adult to help you open and close these pieces of equipment using a pair of fine-nosed pliers or jewellery pliers.

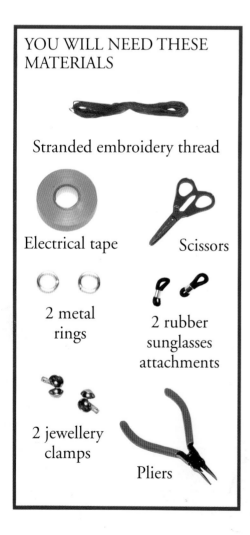

YOU WILL NEED THESE MATERIALS

Stranded embroidery thread

Electrical tape

Scissors

2 metal rings

2 rubber sunglasses attachments

2 jewellery clamps

Pliers

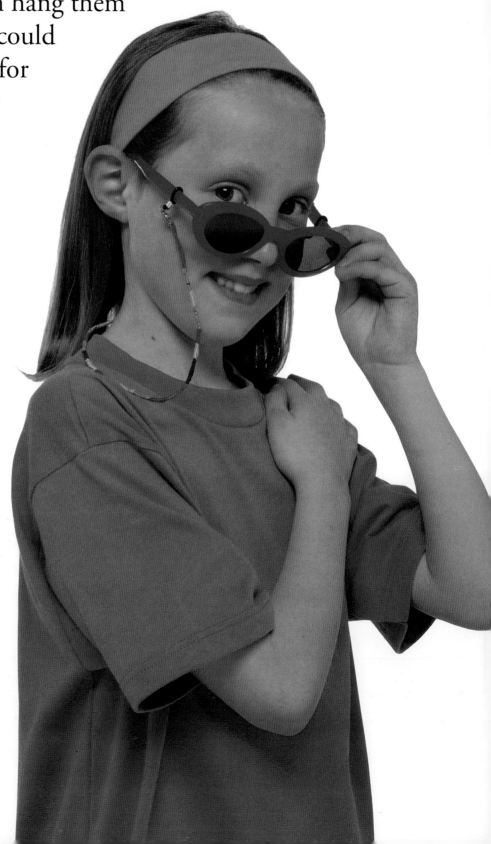

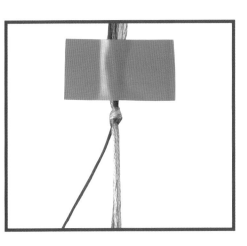

1 Cut six strands of thread, each 200cm (80in) long. Knot the threads together, 5cm (2in) from the top. Tape them to the work surface.

2 Take the red thread that is out on its own and put it over the other threads, then under them and through the loop. Pull the thread up tightly.

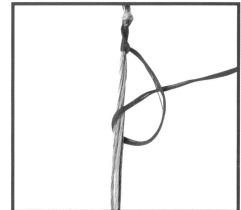

3 Continue knotting this single thread over the others until you have as much as you want of that colour and want to change it.

4 Take a new thread and place the red thread with the others. Make a row of knots as shown in step 2. Continue knotting in this way and changing the thread colour as often as you wish.

5 When the knotted cord is about 70cm (28in) long, tie the threads in a tight knot close to the braid. Trim the loose threads very close to the knot at each end. Take care that you do not cut into the knots themselves.

Using other styles of braid

Many of the other braiding techniques shown can also be used to make the Sunglasses Strap. Whichever Friendship Bracelet design you choose, allow at least 200cm (80in) of each thread. If you choose to make a wide strap, you may need to use larger jewellery clamps and metal rings.

6 Attach a jewellery clamp over each knot and close the clamps. Attach a metal ring to each clamp and a rubber loop to each ring.

To attach the strap, thread the rubber loops over the arms of your sunglasses and tighten the loops around the arms.

Boxes and Bands Bracelet

This is quite a difficult bracelet to make. If you are not pleased with your first attempt, keep practising until you become an expert.

Handy hint

Use only two different coloured threads for this bracelet. If you use more, the clever boxes and bands design will not stand out.

YOU WILL NEED THESE MATERIALS

Soft embroidery thread

Electrical tape

Scissors

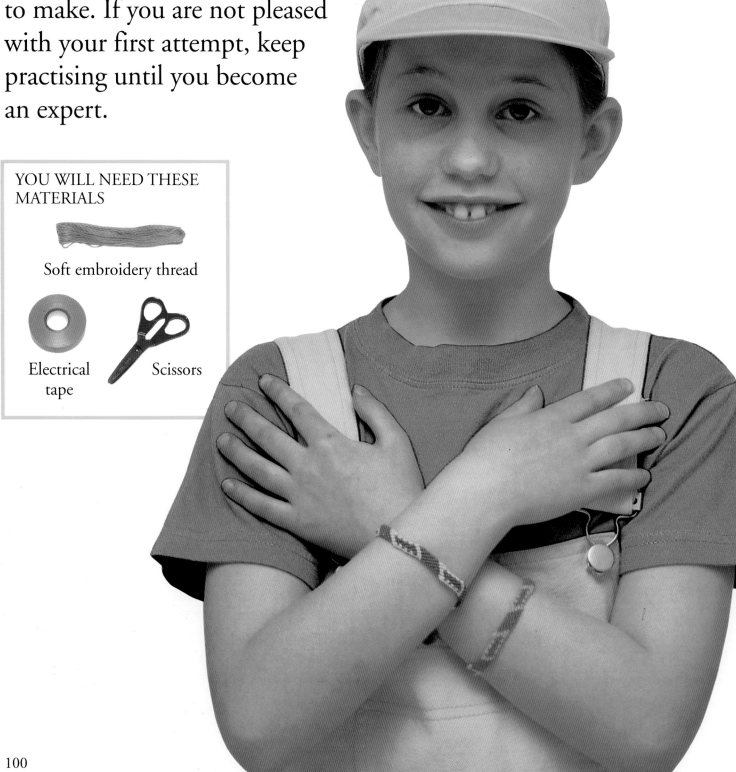

1 Cut two threads in one colour and four in another colour, each 100cm (40in) long. Knot threads and plait for 5cm (2in). Tape threads to work surface.

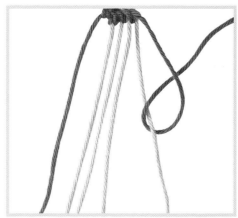

2 Arrange threads as shown in step 1. Knot the far left thread (dark blue) over the threads to the right. Do two knots on each thread.

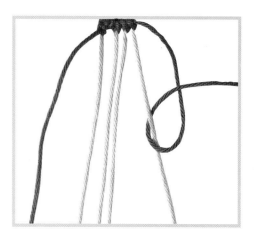

3 Knot the far left thread (also dark blue) over the pale blue thread and do two knots. Repeat, knotting the far right thread over the thread to the left.

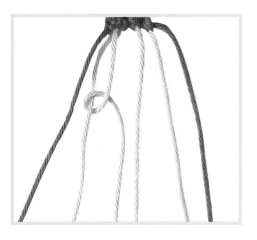

4 Knot the pale blue thread (second on the left) over the thread to the right. Do two knots. Then do one knot over each of the other pale blue threads.

5 Repeat steps 3 and 4 until you have woven four rows of pale blue threads inside a box of dark blue threads. Take care to braid the right thread each time.

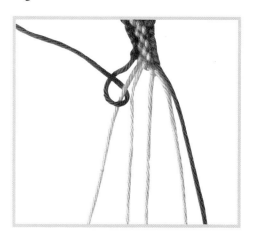

6 Take the dark blue thread on the left and knot it over the pale blue thread next to it. Do two knots and return the thread to the starting position. Do the same with the dark blue thread on the far right.

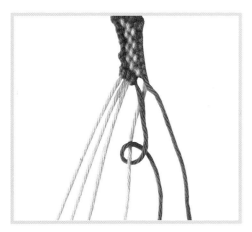

7 Knot the far left dark blue thread over all the threads on the right. Now knot the far left pale blue thread over all the threads on the right until you get to the end of the row.

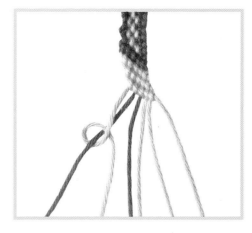

8 Continue knotting the far left thread over the other threads until there is a dark blue thread on either side of the pale blue threads. Repeat steps 2 to 8 until the bracelet is the right length.

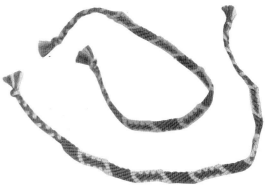

To finish your Boxes and Bands Bracelet, plait 5cm (2in) and then tie the threads into a knot. Trim the threads at both ends to the same length.

Arrow Bracelet

You can make the Arrow Bracelet using two, three or four different coloured threads. Choose colours to match your best outfit or, if you are making this for a friend, choose his or her favourite colours. To make a thicker Arrow Bracelet, use more threads.

YOU WILL NEED THESE MATERIALS

Soft embroidery thread

Electrical tape

Scissors

1 Cut eight pieces of thread, four of each colour and each 100cm (40in) long. Knot the threads 5cm (2in) from the top and tape threads to your work surface. Lay the threads out, as shown.

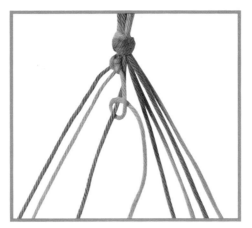

2 Start with the thread on the far left (in this project it is orange) and do two knots on each of the three threads next to it on the right. Leave the orange thread in the middle.

3 Now take the orange thread on the far right and do two knots on each of the three threads next to it on the left. Leave the orange thread in the middle.

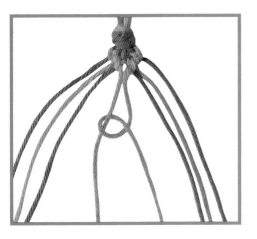

4 Take the middle right orange thread and make two knots over the orange thread on the left.

5 Repeat steps 2, 3 and 4, knotting blue and orange alternately until the bracelet is the right length.

6 Plait the threads for 5cm (2in) and secure with a knot. Trim any uneven threads with scissors.

Give your Arrow Bracelet a finishing touch by threading large beads on to both ends. Make sure that the hole in the beads will allow eight threads to pass through.

Fabulous Hairstyles

Jacki Wadeson

Introduction

Doing your hair is such fun, and you will be surprised to see how easy it is to create different styles. There are lots of things you can do whether your hair is straight, wavy or curly, short or long. All you need is a brush and comb, and as many brightly coloured ribbons, beads, bows, covered bands and fancy hair clips as you can find.

Getting started

Firstly, assemble all the materials and accessories you will need. Then find somewhere to set up your hair salon. Ideally you need a table, chair and a large mirror. Ask for permission before you start rearranging furniture and also ask an adult to help set up a mirror, if necessary.

It is also a good idea to ask a friend to join you. A friend can not only do the plaits and ponytails at the back of your head, your friend can also tell you just how wonderful you look with your new hairstyle. Having your own hair done is only half the fun – the other half is doing someone else's hair!

Basic techniques

Before you start on the exotic hair styles like Crimping Crazy, Wonder Waves and Beaded Plaits, it is a good idea to practise the basic techniques. The basic techniques include the Perfect Ponytail, High Ponytail, Bouncy Bunches and the Simple Plait. When you have mastered these, then even the most

This style uses the basic techniques to create a simply spectacular look. The ribbons are the final touch!

Mini plaits look great with beads threaded on to the end.

complicated styles will be easy to do.

It is also important that you comb and brush your hair correctly. Tugging and pulling roughly on your hair will only damage it. Brush your hair with a gentle brush to smooth it and to make it easy to style. To remove knots or tangles, use a wide-toothed comb. Separate out the section of tangled hair and start combing from below the tangle and gradually work your way up the section of hair until the tangle disappears. Never try to force a comb through a knot from above – it will tear your hair.

Making a centre or side parting in your hair is easy with a wide-toothed comb, but making the parting straight requires practice. Your hairstyles will look really professional if the parting does not wiggle around like a snake!

Everyone's hair is different and some hair types are better suited to some hair styles. To work out which styles work best for you is simply a matter of trial and error. If you have flyaway hair, for example, cover a bristle brush with a silk scarf and stroke it over the hair. The static electricity that makes hair wispy will magically disappear. To flatten hair that sticks up, wet your hands with water and smooth them over your hair.

Materials

Here are the materials and equipment you will need to set up your hair salon. To create the hairstyles, you do not need a hairdryer or any type of hair gel or lotion. If you go on to create other hair designs and need things like a hairdryer or hair gel, always ask an adult for permission.

Beads Plaiting, or braiding, beads have a large hole through which a fine plait can be threaded. They come in lots of different colours and can be bought in craft and hobby shops.

Brush You will need a brush with widely spaced soft bristles. The bristles can be made from nylon or a natural fibre. Keep your brush clean by running a comb through it to remove hairs. Some brushes can be washed under running water. It is always best to have your own brush and comb.

Covered bands You need lots of these towelling or yarn covered stretchy bands. Unlike ordinary rubber bands, these bands will not damage your hair. They come in lots of different sizes, thicknesses, colours and textures. You can buy inexpensive packets of assorted covered bands in supermarkets, department stores and chemists.

Fabric curlers These soft curlers are easy to use and much more comfortable to wear than other types of curlers. You can buy them in department stores and chemist shops.

Hairband Use one of these to keep your hair off your face. All hairbands are made of flexible plastic, but some are padded with a soft material and covered in fabric, cord or ribbon.

Hair grips These are sometimes called Kirbigrips or hair slides, and they are used to keep a small section of hair in place. They are made of sprung metal and have plastic, rounded tips so that they do not damage your hair or hurt your scalp. They come in different sizes and colours.

Ribbons You really cannot have too many ribbons when styling your hair. Start collecting ribbons of different widths, colours, textures and patterns.

Scrunchy This is a loop of elastic covered by a wide strip of fabric. You can buy scrunchies in lots of different sizes.

Thick cord To bind a plait you use a thick cord, or cording, that can be bought on rolls or by the metre (yard) in craft and fabric shops. Cord without a shiny, smooth finish is the easiest to use as it will not slide off the plait.

Thread To put beads on to plaits you will need to use a thick thread like an embroidery thread. Embroidery threads or similar come in lots of colours. There is even a glittery thread.

Wide-toothed comb This comb has large spaces between the teeth and is good for untangling knots. Always rinse after use.

Wide-toothed comb

Small covered band

Thick cord

Beads

Thread

Hairband

Fabric curler

Large covered band

Scrunchy

Hair grips

Yarn-covered bands

Ribbon

Brush

Accessories

Hair accessories are used to decorate your hair rather than to create a style. They are the finishing touch to ponytails, plaits and bunches. Even a simple hair clip can turn an ordinary plait into something special.

Chemist shops and department stores are full of colourful and beautiful hair accessories. Some are expensive, others are very inexpensive. When choosing a hair accessory make sure that it is the right sort for your hair and for what you want it to do. Some hair slides and grips, for example, are made for long or thick hair; others for fine or short hair. Always try to select hair accessories that will coordinate with your favourite outfits or with other hair accessories you want to use.

You do not even need to buy special hair accessories, you can design and make your own using all sorts of unusual materials. Pictured below are hair accessories decorated with uninflated balloons, fabric flowers from a florist, tiny ribbon flowers from a haberdashery shop, and varnished sweets.

Here are some other unusual materials that you could use when designing and decorating your own unique range of hair accessories: colourful raffia, string, shells, beads, embroidery thread, papier mâché, tiny toys and dolls, crêpe paper (but do not get it wet), plastic bags, gift-wrapping ribbon, strips of leftover fabric, and dried pulses and pasta.

To start making hair accessories you will need something to decorate (a plastic hairband, a plain plastic-backed hair slide or hair grip), PVA glue and brush, sewing needle and thread, and your imagination. To get you started you could make the Glitzy Hairband on the next page.

If you think that creating fabulous hairstyles is lots of fun, wait till you start making your own hair accessories!

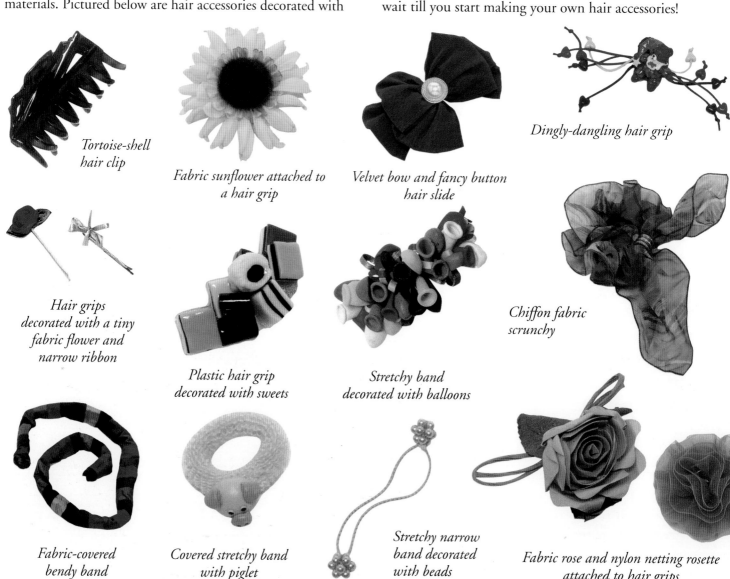

Tortoise-shell hair clip

Fabric sunflower attached to a hair grip

Velvet bow and fancy button hair slide

Dingly-dangling hair grip

Hair grips decorated with a tiny fabric flower and narrow ribbon

Plastic hair grip decorated with sweets

Stretchy band decorated with balloons

Chiffon fabric scrunchy

Fabric-covered bendy band

Covered stretchy band with piglet

Stretchy narrow band decorated with beads

Fabric rose and nylon netting rosette attached to hair grips

Glitzy Hairband

Create your own designer hair accessory by simply sewing an assortment of brightly coloured beads on to a padded hairband.

YOU WILL NEED THESE MATERIALS

Felt

Padded hairband

Scissors

PVA glue and brush

Tiny and small beads

Beading needle and sewing thread

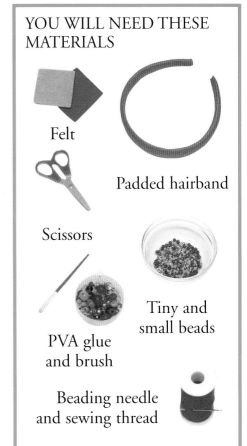

1 Cut out small dots of felt in lots of different colours. Dab a small spot of glue on to the padded hairband where you want each dot to be. Stick the felt dots on and let the glue dry.

2 Carefully sew a bead on to the centre of each felt dot. Do two or three stitches. Then knot the thread around the bead. Cut the thread as close as possible to the knot. Do the same for all the remaining beads.

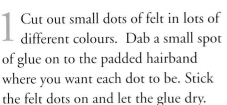

3 To make a different style of hairband, select a mixture of beads that match the colour of the hairband, or create a rainbow effect by sewing your beads in rows of one colour. Use sparkly beads and a black hairband to make a special occasion hairband.

Perfect Ponytail

A ponytail is one of the easiest styles to do. It keeps hair tidy and stops it getting into a tangle when playing sports or swimming.

1 Brush your hair straight back off your face using long sweeping strokes to make sure there are no knots. Tease any knots out by brushing gently from the bottom.

2 Place the scrunchy around your wrist. Pull your hair together with your hands at the back of your head. Your hair should go over the top of your ears.

Hair care hint

Scrunchies are very good for holding your hair in place because they do not tear or damage the hair. Ordinary rubber bands can tear your hair when they are removed. If you have very silky or fine hair, it may be necessary to hold the hair in place with a small, yarn-covered elastic before finishing with a large, colourful scrunchy.

3 Hold your hair in place using the hand on which the scrunchy is wound. Use the other hand to slip the scrunchy off the wrist and over the ponytail. Keep holding the hair while the scrunchy is twisted, as shown.

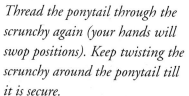

Thread the ponytail through the scrunchy again (your hands will swop positions). Keep twisting the scrunchy around the ponytail till it is secure.

High Ponytail

A high ponytail, right on the top of your head, makes you instantly taller. This is a glam style that is great for parties and discos.

YOU WILL NEED

Brush

3 scrunchies

2 hair grips   2 fabric flowers

1 Tip your head forwards and brush your hair from the back of your neck right to the ends. Make sure there are no tangles or knots. It is easiest if you use a brush with wide spaces between the bristles.

2 Take hold of your hair with one hand. Run the fingers of your other hand through your hair to make it smooth. Hold your hair and lift your head up.

3 Put a scrunchy over the knuckles of one hand, then pull your hair though the scrunchy. Twist the band and pull your hair through again. Repeat until the scrunchy holds your hair securely.

4 Twist on two more scrunchies above the first one. These will give your ponytail lots of height and make you look really tall. You can use scrunchies in matching or contrasting colours.

To finish, use hair grips to pin the fabric flowers in place. You can buy fabric or net flowers in the sewing departments of large stores or in craft shops.

Pony Princess

Here the top section of your hair is smoothed back into a ponytail halfway down the back of your head. It is then combined with the rest of your hair to make another ponytail.

Handy hint

A fabric-covered bendy band is made from a long flexible strip of wire that is sewn into the edge of a strip of fabric. To make the topknot in the band, put the band around your head and then twist the the ends together.

YOU WILL NEED

Brush

4 covered bands

Fabric-covered bendy band

You can wear your Pony Princess ponytail hanging down your back or, if you have very long hair, draped over your shoulder.

1 Brush your hair so there are no tangles or knots. Then use your thumbs to divide off the top section of your hair, as shown. Hold this section tightly with one hand.

2 Use a towelling-covered band to secure this top section of hair. You may need to twist the band once or twice so that it is tight enough to hold the hair properly.

3 Gather all your hair together at the nape of your neck and secure it in another towelling band of a different colour. You may need to twist it again so it is tight enough to stay in place.

4 Take another coloured band and do the same thing again. The bands should sit neatly next to one another, so push them together.

5 Add another coloured band about halfway down the ponytail. Brush or comb the end of the ponytail to make it smooth.

To finish, place a fabric-covered bendy band round the back of your head. The band can go over or under the ponytail. Bring the ends of the band to the front of your head. Twist the ends together to make a topknot

Topsy Turvy Ponytail

A topknot is great if you are growing out your fringe because it can catch all those little ends that tend to stick out or fall over your eyes.

Handy hint

Twist the ribbons together for a really unusual hairband, and choose colours that match your clothes. To stop the ribbons slipping, it may be necessary to secure them with small hair grips placed just behind each ear.

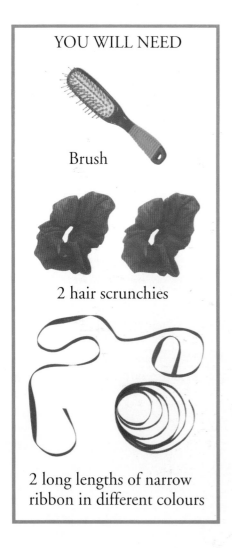

YOU WILL NEED

Brush

2 hair scrunchies

2 long lengths of narrow ribbon in different colours

1 Brush your hair through to remove any tangles or knots. Use the thumb of each hand to divide off the top section of the hair from your ears up to the top of your head.

2 Push a scrunchy or other type of fabric-covered band over the fingers of one hand so that it rests on your knuckles. Clasp the topknot of hair in your other hand.

3 Slip the scrunchy over the hair. Twist the scrunchy and then pull the ponytail through the scrunchy. Repeat until the scrunchy holds the hair securely.

4 Add a second scrunchy and twist it around the top of the first scrunchy. This will give the Topsy Turvy Ponytail height. If the first scrunchy was large and thick, you may not need to add a second scrunchy.

For an extra-special touch, dress up your topknot by wrapping two long lengths of narrow ribbon around your head like a hairband. Secure the ribbons by tying the ends under your hair at the back of your neck. This looks best when the ribbons are of different colours.

Bouncy Bunches

YOU WILL NEED

Comb

2 covered bands

Two lengths of ribbon

Fairy bows on hair grips

Any length of hair can be scooped up into pretty bunches. Tie the bunches with bright ribbons in fun colours and patterns for school, and add fairy bows for party time.

1 Part your hair in the middle from front to back. Put a covered band over one hand, so that it sits on your knuckles. Hold one half of your hair in the other hand.

2 Slip the bunch through the covered band, holding your hair tightly with one hand. Use your thumb to pull the band tight and then twist it.

3 Put your fingers through the loop in the band and pull the bunch through. Do this again until the band is tight enough to hold your hair.

4 Tie a short piece of ribbon round the bunch, then make a bow. Repeat for the other side. To finish, slide two fairy bows on either side of the centre parting at the front.

Banded Bunches

Keep your bunches tidy by wrapping bands of colour round them all the way to the bottom. Finish off your hairstyle with a pair of madcap decorated bands.

1 Part your hair in the middle from front to back. Put a plain band over one hand so it sits on your knuckles, then slip it over one section of hair. Twist it back over the bunch until it is tight. Repeat for the other bunch.

2 Take two bands (we used ones decorated with piglets) and slip one over each bunch. You may need to twist the bands twice so that they hold each bunch tightly.

3 Take two more plain bands and slip a bunch through each band, about 5cm (2in) from the first band. These bands should be a different colour to the decorated bands.

4 Take more plain bands (in a different colour to the last ones) and add them to your bunches, always about 5cm (2in) from the last band. Continue until you run out of hair or covered bands!

Can you guess what these madcap bands are made from? Lots and lots of small balloons!

117

Be-Bop Bunches

High bunches like these are really easy to do on bobbed or shoulder-length hair. You can twist ribbon around a small section of hair for a really snazzy look!

1 Part your hair in the centre and brush your hair so it is really smooth. Take a small section at one side and brush again. Experiment to see how large a section you would like to use.

2 Tie this small section of hair in a covered band. We used crocheted silky bands in a rainbow of colours. You can use your favourite bands but make sure they are not to thick or large.

3 Twist the band and wrap it around the bunch until it is tight enough to hold the bunch in place. Repeat for the other side.

Hair care tip
To keep your hair shiny after shampooing, always use cool water for the final rinse.

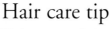

4 Divide off a small section of the hair from one of the bunches and slip the end of the ribbon halfway through the covered band. To keep the ribbon in place, tie it on to the band. Twist the ribbon around your hair and tie the ends in a knot and then a bow.

Teeny Bopper

You can use bouncy curls and waves to create lots of styles. The Teeny Bopper style makes it look as though your hair is much thicker than it really is!

YOU WILL NEED

Brush

3 large covered bands

1 Lift a section of hair from the front to the top of your head, and then use a bristle brush to smooth the front of your hair. Do not brush through the length of your hair or you will pull the waves out.

2 Take a large covered band (one that will wrap round lots of times) and use it to secure the top section of hair. Make sure this is right in the middle, because you do not want your topknot to be lopsided.

3 Separate out a section of hair from one side of your head. Fasten it with another large, covered band in a different colour. Loosen the waves with your fingers, but do not brush your hair.

This girl is ready to dance. When she dances, her curls will bounce and bop!

4 Do exactly the same with a section of hair on the other side of your head. Do not forget to use a different coloured band!

Simple Plait

A three-stranded plait, also called a braid, is a lot easier to do than it looks. Plaits are really useful for keeping your hair under control, especially when swimming.

YOU WILL NEED

Comb

Brush

2 covered bands

1 Part your hair from centre front to the nape of your neck. Divide one half of your hair into three equal sections and hold the back and front outer sections.

2 Cross the back section over the centre section. Use your fingers to make sure that the other two sections remain separate. Pull gently on the back section as you cross it over.

To finish, hold your plait 5cm (2in) from the end. Take a covered band and slip it over the end, then twist it back over as many times as needed to keep the plait secure.

3 Cross the front section over the centre section. Gently pull all three sections evenly as you work, so that the plait is straight.

4 Now you can see how the plait is beginning to form. Carry on plaiting by crossing the back section over the centre section, and the front section over the centre section.

Triple Twist

This is a perfect style if your hair is thick and wavy. A ponytail is divided into three sections and each section is plaited. Then these plaits are braided to make one plait.

YOU WILL NEED

Large, covered band

3 small bands

Brush

Chiffon hair accessory

1 Brush your hair into a low ponytail at the nape of your neck using a wide bristled brush. Make sure the front and sides are really smooth. Secure the ponytail with the large, covered band.

2 Divide the ponytail into three equal sections. Take the first one and plait it from top to bottom. If your hair is long enough, bring the plaits over to the front of your shoulder.

3 When you get to the end of the plait, secure it with a small band. Plait the other two sections in exactly the same way. You now have three plaits to work with.

4 Take the three single plaits and plait them together in the same way as before. Your hair will form into a thick plait that looks like a twist of hair.

To finish, twist a fancy colourful chiffon hair accessory around the plait. If you do not have one, then use a large, covered band to match the one at the top of the plait.

Pretty Plaited Flips

This style is inspired by the North American Indians. In their culture, men and women plait their hair and then bind the plaits with cord.

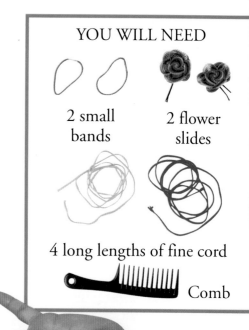

YOU WILL NEED

2 small bands

2 flower slides

4 long lengths of fine cord

Comb

When choosing the cord to bind your plaits, avoid those with a very shiny, smooth finish. These cords are difficult to knot and they will slip off the plait.

1 Part your hair in the centre, and then plait the hair on one side from the roots to the ends. Keep the tension even so that your plait is straight.

2 Secure the end of the plait with a covered band, twisting it back over until it holds the plaits tightly. Do the same with the remaining hair.

3 Take a piece of cord and, starting at the top, bind the plait by wrapping the cord tightly round it. Keep the circles of cord close to one another.

Add flowers or matching slides to either side of your head, at the front or above the plaits.

4 Halfway down the plait, change the colour of the cord. Hold the ends of the first and second colours against the plait and bind the new colour tightly round the ends. Continue binding until you reach the end of the plait.

5 Secure the end of the cord by tucking it into the covered band that holds the plait together.

Racy Ribbons

Plaits look really good if you include ribbons as you go. At the ends, tie each ribbon into a bow for a really beautiful cascade of colour.

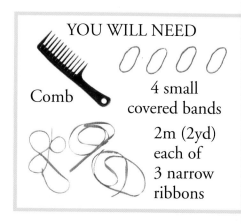

YOU WILL NEED

Comb

4 small covered bands

2m (2yd) each of 3 narrow ribbons

1 Part your hair in the centre and brush it through. Gather up the hair at each side and use a covered band to secure in bunches. Make the bunches at about ear level. Cut the ribbons in half.

2 Take three lengths of ribbon, each of a different colour. Pull the ends halfway through the band, then tie them on to it once. Make sure the ends are even.

3 Divide the hair into three sections and put two matching pieces of ribbon with each one. Plait the hair as normal but include the lengths of ribbon into the plait.

4 Secure the end of the plait, including the ribbons, in a small, covered band. Now take each pair of matching ribbons and tie them in a bow. Plait and tie the other side.

Choose ribbons that match your outfit or show which football team you support.

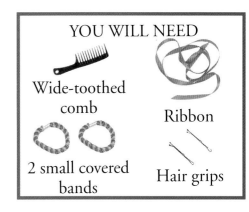

Ribbon Roll

It is easy to make very curly hair look neat and tidy if you plait a high ponytail with ribbon and twirl it into a roll.

YOU WILL NEED

Wide-toothed comb

Ribbon

2 small covered bands

Hair grips

1 Use a comb with widely spaced teeth to help you smooth your hair up on to the top of your head. Hold your hair with one hand and put a small, covered band over the other hand. Twist the band round your hair a number of times to secure the ponytail.

2 Plait the ponytail from the top right down to the ends. Secure the ends with another small, covered band. You could leave your hair just like this if you wanted to.

3 Take a length of the ribbon and slip one end under the covered band at the top of your head and pull through, so the ends are even. Bind the ponytail with the ribbon right down to the ends.

4 Take the ends of the ribbon and plait in one hand and roll the lot round on itself to make a bun. Use one or two hair grips to secure the bun in place. Leave the ends of the ribbon to fall free.

The Ribbon Roll looks very classy. It is the perfect hairstyle for a special occasion like a wedding or fancy party.

125

Beaded Plaits

Fine plaits with beads threaded through the ends look spectacular. Bead just a few plaits around your face or ask a friend to help you do them all over your head.

YOU WILL NEED

Beads

Brush

Thread

Hair grip

Safety!

Make sure you always keep your hair beads in a safe place away from babies or small children, who may think they are sweets.

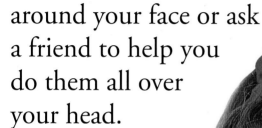

Add colourful beads – as many as you wish – to brighten up your hair.

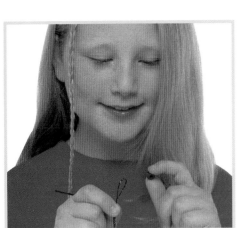

1 Plait a small section of hair down one side of your face. Secure the ends with a hair grip. Fold an 18cm (7in) piece of glittery thread to make a loop.

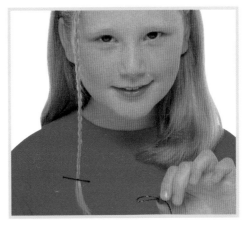

2 Pass the looped end of the glittery thread through the centre of the bead. This is easy if the bead has a large hole in the centre.

3 Remove the hair grip and pass the end of the plait through the loop of thread. Make sure you keep a firm hold on the bead, so that it does not fall off.

4 Push the bead towards the plait, then pull on the ends of the thread. This will pull the plait through the hole in the bead. Continue pulling until the end of the plait comes through the bead.

5 Wrap the thread round and round the end of the plait, making sure the strands lie flat. Carry on until you have covered about 1cm (1/2in) of hair below the bead.

Beads galore!

To put more than one bead on each plait, complete up to step 4 and then thread another bead on to the glittery thread. Push the bead towards the plait and then pull on the thread so that the plait comes through the hole in the bead. Repeat as many time as you like before following steps 5 and 6.

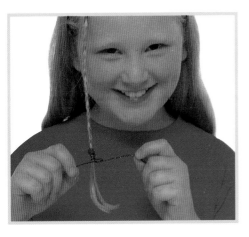

6 Cross over the ends of the thread, then tie a tight knot close to the plait. Trim the threads but be careful not to trim your hair!

Beaded plaits look best if the beads on each plait are level.

Plaits and Bows

Simple plaits can be tied at the back of the head in a pretty bow, while tiny front plaits can be decorated with small beads.

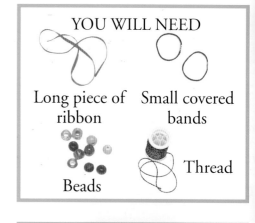

YOU WILL NEED

Long piece of ribbon   Small covered bands

Beads   Thread

1 Part your hair in the centre, then take a small section of hair from one side. Start plaiting near the roots and work all the way down to the ends. Secure the ends with a covered band.

2 Take a small section of hair from the other side of your head and plait in the same way. Secure the ends in a covered band, twisting and wrapping the band round until it holds tight.

3 Take the braids round to the centre of the back of your head. Tie them together with a long piece of ribbon and loop it into a bow. Leave the ribbon ends dangling.

4 Plait two more sections of hair, so that each one hangs in front of an ear. Thread three different-coloured beads on to each plait (see Beaded Plaits). Try to match some of the beads to the colour of the ribbon.

In place of the ribbon bow you can tie back the plaits with a fancy scrunchy or decorative covered band.

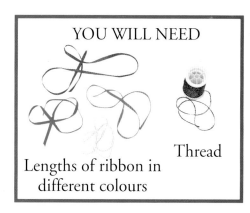

Bound Plaits

Medium-length or long straight hair can be plaited then wrapped with different coloured ribbons for a really wild style.

YOU WILL NEED

Lengths of ribbon in different colours

Thread

Take small sections of hair and plait them tightly from roots to ends. You may need a friend to help you plait the hair at the back.

2 Secure the end of each plait by winding fine, colourful thread two or three times around each plait. Secure with a firm knot and trim threads.

Handy hint

For each plait you will need a length of narrow ribbon that is three times the length of the plait.

3 Fold a length of ribbon in half. Tie the ribbon to the top of the plait. The ends should be even. Bind the plait by crossing the lengths of ribbon over and over, first at the front of the braid, then at the back.

Continue binding until you reach the end of the plait. Tie the ends of the ribbon in a tight knot. Repeat until you have bound all your plaits. You will need a friend to help you bind the plaits at the back of your head.

129

Crimping Crazy

You do not need a crimping iron gadget to create soft ripples in your hair – all you have to do is plait your hair in lots of fine plaits. You will need to leave the plaits in overnight to set so do not leave this fabulous hairstyle to the last minute!

Hair care hint

When unravelling the plaits be gentle and patient. If you pull roughly on your hair you will damage it. Untangle any knots by starting at the hair ends and working upwards with a wide-toothed comb.

If you use only a wide-toothed comb on your crimps, they should last until you next wash your hair.

YOU WILL NEED

Wide-toothed comb

Thread

Hairband

Fabric flowers

1 Divide your hair into fine sections and braid it from the roots to the ends, making the plaits even and quite tight. The smaller the sections are, the finer the finished crimp will be.

2 Secure the end of each plait with a piece of thread, wrap it around two or three times and then tie the ends into a little knot. If you prefer, you can use very small covered bands.

3 Leave the plaits in overnight to set your hair into lots of soft ripples. You can lightly mist your hair with water if you wish but do not go to bed with wet hair.

4 In the morning carefully unravel each braid, loosening it with your fingers as you go.

5 You can leave your hair loose and flowing or keep it off your face with a hairband. For a special occasion make two small ponytails at the front and tie on fabric flowers with cord or ribbon.

Wonder Waves

Straight hair can be changed into a mass of waves by using fabric curlers. You can leave the curlers in overnight, but even after a few hours you can achieve wonderful results.

Handy hint

You will get tighter and curlier Wonder Waves if your hair is just slightly damp when you put the curlers in. The easiest way to dampen your hair is with a water mist sprayer, but ask for permission before you borrow one. Never go to bed with wet hair.

YOU WILL NEED

Lots of fabric curlers

Fabric flower   Brush

To make your lustrous locks look even more wonderful, tie a small ponytail at the top of your head. Secure with a covered band and use a hair grip to pin a brilliant fabric flower to the front of the ponytail. Fan out the ponytail so that it falls naturally around the sides and back of your head.

1 Take a fabric curler and fold it in half to grip a section of hair between the two pieces. Pull the curler right down to the bottom of the hair.

2 Wind the fabric curler up the hair from the ends towards your head. Do this slowly and make sure you do not let go of either end of the curler.

3 When you can wind no further, hold the ends of the curler and bring them together. Cross the ends over to lock the curler in place.

4 Repeat all over your head. Remember, the bigger the sections of hair you wind, the looser the wave will be. For really tight curls, take only small sections and use lots of curlers.

To reveal your Wonder Waves, gently undo and remove each curler. Use your fingers to 'rake' through each wave. You will look amazing!

5 Leave your curlers in overnight. They are very soft, so they are comfortable to sleep in.

Fancy Dress Masks

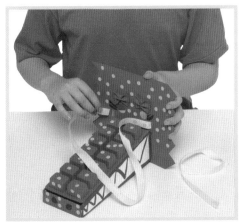

Thomasina Smith

Introduction

Masks are used to transform people and for disguise. In many ancient cultures, masks were an important part of religious and social customs. The person wearing the mask could become a god or a spirit. But masks are also important in modern culture. They are used in the re-enactment of special events, in the theatre and for fun. Japanese theatre relies on the actors wearing masks to portray certain characters, and could you imagine a street carnival without people wearing funny masks? There are even special parties, called masquerade balls, to which everyone must wear a mask.

You can make a mask to wear to a party, for dressing-up or to wear in a school play. Masks also make great wall decorations. The Fancy Dress Masks that follow are both easy and fun to make. Card, fabric and papier-mâché are good basic materials, but you can also use items such as an ice-cube tray, an old tennis ball or pan scrubbers. In fact, almost anything can be used in mask-making. Following are some basic techniques that will help you to make some wonderful masks.

The very scary Wicke Witch mas

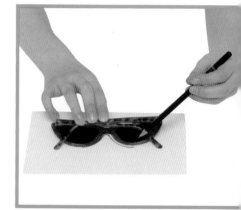

The Venetian Mask makes the wearer look most mysterious.

Fitting a mask

To make eye and mouth holes in the right positions on your mask, you need to know the distance between your eyes and the distance from your nose to your mouth. Start out by tracing around a pair of glasses or swimming goggles on to your mask. Then measure the distance from the bridge of your nose to your mouth. Measure and mark this distance on your mask.

Cutting eye holes

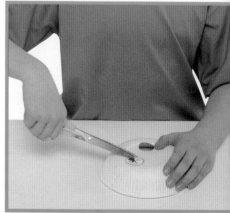

1 Hold a paper plate in front of your face. Carefully feel where your eyes are using your fingers.

2 When you have found where your eyes are, mark the position of each one on the paper plate with a pencil.

3 Draw two circles around the marks. Make a hole in the centre of the circles, then cut around the outlines.

Cutting a mouth

To cut out a mouth from a paper plate or card mask is easy if you do this simple trick.

Draw the outline of the mouth on to the back of a paper plate or card. Fold the mask in half so that the centre of the mouth is on the fold. Cut across the fold, following your outline. This will make sure that the cut-out mouth is even on both sides of your mask.

This mask is two masks in one. Open out the Hungry Wolf mask to reveal the Unlucky Lamb.

Attaching straps and ties

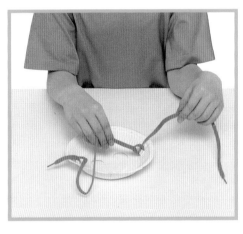

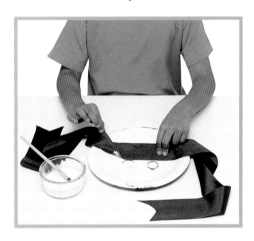

1 Cut two small holes on each side of the mask. Attach a strap to one side and place the mask on your face. Run the strap around the back of your head. Pinch the strap with your fingers when it makes contact with the second side.

2 Take the mask off, but do not let go of the strap – keep it pinched between your fingers. Put a mark on the strap where it is pinched between your fingers. Thread the strap through the second side and tie firmly at the mark.

3 Another way of attaching a strap is to glue it to the back of the mask. Mark the middle of a 1m (1yd) long strap and position the mark in the centre of the mask just below the eye holes. Allow to dry before wearing the mask.

There is something very fishy about this mask.

Safety tips

❖ Keep glues, sharp utensils and pointed objects well out of the reach of young children.

❖ Never put sharp or pointed objects near your eyes. When trying on a mask for the first time, check that there is no wet paint or glue on the back of the mask. Also check that there are no sharp edges. It is a good idea to stick clear sticky tape around the edges of masks made with a foil baking trays. Put tape around eye, nose and mouth holes as well.

❖ Plastic food wrap and plastic bags should never be used to decorate a mask.

❖ Ask an adult to trim the points and remove splinters from wooden skewers or garden sticks before using.

Materials

These are the main materials and items you will need to complete the Fancy Dress Mask projects.

Basket A round, cane or straw basket is best. It should be about the same size as a large plate.

Cotton wool You can use either cotton wool balls or a roll of cotton wool.

Corrugated card This thick brown card has ripples on one side and is smooth on the other. For some projects you can use corrugated card recycled from boxes. Other projects require a large sheet of corrugated card. It can be purchased in rolls or sheets from stationery and craft shops.

Disposable kitchenware This includes things like paper plates, plastic cups and foil baking trays or pie plates. Some of these items can be recycled from empty food packaging.

Fabric You can use a large piece of leftover plain or printed fabric or buy an inexpensive remnant from a fabric shop.

Funnel A small plastic funnel is available from hardware and kitchen shops. It can be used to make a nose for a mask.

Ice-cube tray Even an everyday item like a rectangular, plastic ice-cube tray is invaluable in mask-making. As you will not be able to reuse the tray, use an unwanted tray or buy one.

Newspaper You need sheets of newspaper to cover your work surface, and strips of newspaper for making papier-mâché.

Pan scrubber This is a round pad of twisted plastic or metal thread that is used to clean pots and pans. You can buy it in lots of bright colours or in a shiny copper or silver colour.

Pipe-cleaners You can find pipe-cleaners in art and craft shops. They come in various lengths and colours. To make the masks, you need an assortment of coloured, stripy and glittery ones.

Shoelaces These are used to make ties for your masks. You can paint or buy shoelaces to match the colour of your mask.

Sponge Use a felt-tip pen to mark out the shape you want on an ordinary bath or kitchen sponge, then trim with scissors.

String You will need fine, plain or coloured string to make ties for your masks.

Swimming goggles If you do not already have any swimming goggles, they are easy to find at sports shops. Goggles are fun to use in a mask, and make a cheap substitute for safety goggles too. Wear goggles whenever you are cutting something that may fly up into your eyes.

Tap hose This is used on the end of a kitchen tap to direct the stream of water. You can buy a plastic tap hose in a hardware or kitchen shop. Use it to make a nose for a mask.

Tennis ball If you are making a large mask, such as the Spanish Giant, an old tennis ball cut in half and painted makes a great pair of eyes. Ask an adult to help you cut the tennis ball, as it can be quite tricky to do.

Sponge

Basket

Swimming goggles

Pipe-cleaners

Corrugated card

Newspaper

Disposable kitchenware

Fabric

Shoelaces

Ice-cube tray

Cotton wool

String

Tennis ball

Funnel

Tap hose

Pan scrubber

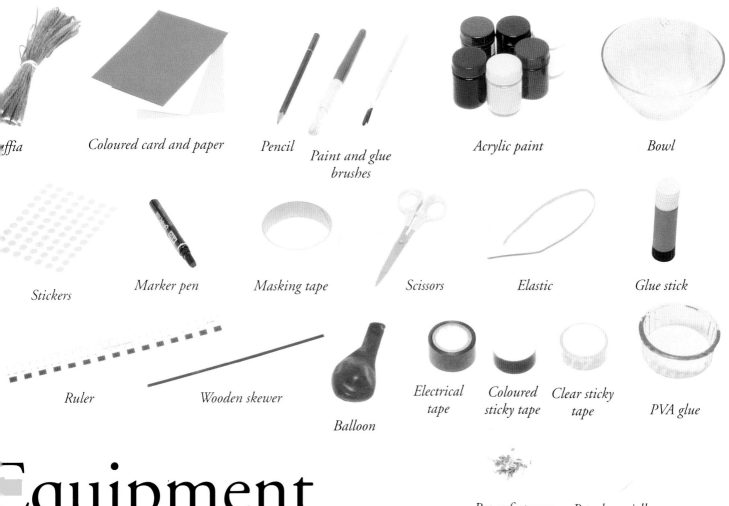

Raffia

Coloured card and paper

Pencil

Paint and glue brushes

Acrylic paint

Bowl

Stickers

Marker pen

Masking tape

Scissors

Elastic

Glue stick

Ruler

Wooden skewer

Balloon

Electrical tape

Coloured sticky tape

Clear sticky tape

PVA glue

Paper fasteners

Petroleum jelly

Equipment

Acrylic paint This is a water-based paint that comes in lots of bright colours. You can also use poster paints.

Balloon You will need an ordinary round balloon to use as a mould for making a papier-mâché mask.

Coloured card and paper Use either scraps of leftover card or paper, or buy sheets from a stationery shop.

Elastic To tie a mask firmly around your head you can use a length of narrow elastic. This can be bought in fabric shops. In place of elastic, use shoelaces, string or ribbon.

Electrical tape This is also called insulating tape, and it can be bought in hardware shops. It comes in various widths and in lots of bright colours.

Glue stick This is great for sticking a piece of paper to a flat surface. Smooth out lumps before leaving it to dry. Always replace the lid, as glue sticks dry out.

Masking tape This is useful for holding things in place while glued surfaces dry. Masking tape can be painted over.

Paper fasteners These are small, shiny metal pins with a round head and two legs. When the legs are pushed through paper or other items and opened, they fasten the items together.

Petroleum jelly This white or creamy jelly is very greasy. It is applied to a balloon before it is covered with papier-mâché. It prevents the papier-mâché from sticking to the balloon.

PVA glue This glue is also known as wood glue, school glue or white glue. PVA glue is a strong glue that can be used to bind paper, card, fabric, plastic or wood surfaces.

Raffia This flat, ribbon-like material is made from the leaves of a palm tree. It comes in tied-up bundles and in lots of bright colours. Buy it in craft shops or stationery shops.

Scissors If possible, you should have two pairs of scissors, one for cutting fabric and the other for cutting paper.

Stickers Use stickers in all sorts of colours, shapes and sizes as a quick way of decorating a mask.

Sticky tapes You can use clear, coloured or patterned sticky tapes to make Fancy Dress Masks.

Wooden skewers These narrow, round, pointed sticks are about 30cm (12in) long and can be bought in supermarkets. You can also use garden sticks or split canes, but ask an adult to cut them to the required length.

Basket Tiger

The idea for this mask is inspired by traditional African masks, many of which looked like wild animals. Just like a real African mask, this mask is made using a natural material – a basket made from cane. Clay and wood were also used to make masks.

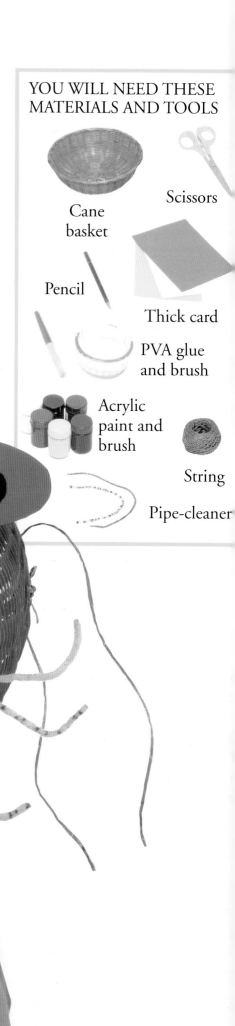

YOU WILL NEED THESE
MATERIALS AND TOOLS

Cane
basket

Scissors

Pencil

Thick card

PVA glue
and brush

Acrylic
paint and
brush

String

Pipe-cleaner

Cut a round hole in the bottom of the basket using a pair of scissors. You may need to ask an adult to help you do this. When cutting the hole, do not put your fingers under the basket.

2 Place the basket on the sheet of coloured card. Draw around the hole. This will become the face of the tiger. Remove the basket and draw an ear on either side of the face.

3 Cut out the face and ears. Draw and cut out a nose from a scrap of thick cardboard. Glue the nose on to the face and leave to dry. Draw, then cut out eye and mouth holes.

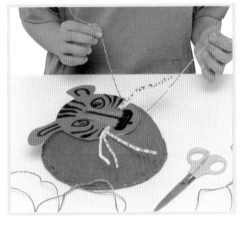

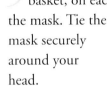

Basket animals

A cane or straw basket and card can be used to make a whole zoo of animals. Follow the instructions for Basket Tiger but modify the face, ears, nose and colouring to make a monkey, a lion, an elephant or a bear. Basket masks would be perfect to use in a school play.

4 Apply glue to the back of the face and press it firmly in position over the hole in the basket. Leave to dry. Paint the basket and face orange. When dry, paint the tiger's features with black paint. Glue pipe-cleaners on either side of the nose for whiskers. Allow the glue to dry thoroughly before starting the next step.

5 Thread string through gaps in the basket, on each side of the mask. Tie the mask securely around your head.

The Basket Tiger mask is easy and quick to make. To act like a real tiger you must growl and move quietly with great stealth.

Venetian Mask

Venice is famous for its Carnival, when everyone dresses up in colourful costumes and fancy masks. This mask is not tied around your head – it is simply fixed to a wooden stick. A Venetian lady would hold the mask to her face when she wanted to be mysterious, and lower it to reveal her beauty.

Handy hint

If you find that PVA glue is not strong enough to hold the wooden skewer securely to the mask, use sticky tape or masking tape as well. It is also a good idea to wind tape around the bottom and the top of the skewer to keep the pipe-cleaners in place.

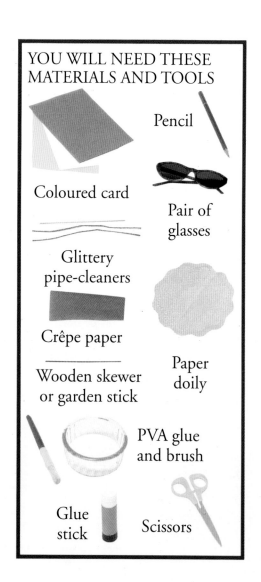

YOU WILL NEED THESE MATERIALS AND TOOLS

Coloured card

Pencil

Pair of glasses

Glittery pipe-cleaners

Crêpe paper

Wooden skewer or garden stick

Paper doily

PVA glue and brush

Glue stick

Scissors

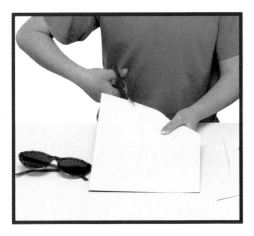

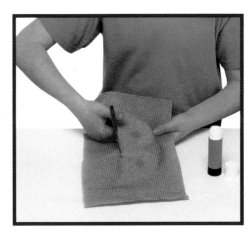

1 Place a pair of glasses on to the card and draw around them with a pencil. Add on to your outline the fancy curves on both sides of the mask. Cut out the card with scissors.

2 Apply glue to the front of the card with the brush and place a large piece of crêpe paper on top. Smooth out the crêpe paper. When the glue is dry, trim around the edges with scissors.

3 Fold the paper doily in half and cut out the semi-circle in the middle. Unfold the doily and cut in half following the fold line. Pleat one half of the doily so that it looks like a fan.

Safety!

Be careful when moving around wearing a mask. Your vision may be restricted by the size of eye holes in the mask. Take extra care when there are wooden sticks attached to the mask.

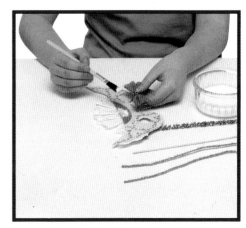

4 Glue the other half of the doily to the front of the mask with paper glue. The cut-out semi-circle should be at the top of the mask. Trim around the edges so that it fits the mask perfectly. Glue the pleated doily to the top of the mask. Draw eye holes on to the front of the mask, then cut them out.

5 Ask an adult to trim any sharp ends from the wooden skewer or garden stick. Tightly wind pipe-cleaners around the skewer to cover it completely. Fix the skewer to the back of the mask with PVA glue and leave to dry thoroughly. Cut a rectangle of crêpe paper and wind a pipe-cleaner around the middle to make a bow. Glue the bow on to the mask, as shown. Allow to dry.

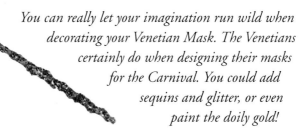

You can really let your imagination run wild when decorating your Venetian Mask. The Venetians certainly do when designing their masks for the Carnival. You could add sequins and glitter, or even paint the doily gold!

Easter Rabbit

Make this fun rabbit mask to wear on Easter morning. Its plump, white cheeks are made from bath sponges. To make the whiskers you can use wooden skewers or plastic straws.

YOU WILL NEED THESE MATERIALS AND TOOLS

Pipe-cleaners   Coloured card

Scissors

Pencil

PVA glue and brush

Glue stick

Black felt-tip pen

Two bath sponges

Six wooden skewers or plastic straws

Small pieces of black and white paper

Ruler

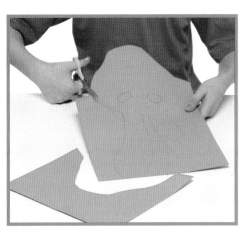

1 Draw and cut out a rabbit's face and ears, measuring 30cm (12in) wide and 60cm (24in) long, from thin coloured card. Cut out two eye holes.

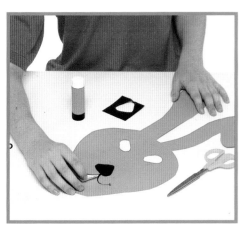

3 Draw a mouth with the felt-tip pen. Cut out a nose from black paper and a pair of teeth from white paper. Glue them on to the mask.

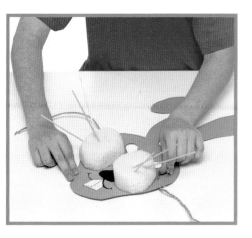

5 Make a small hole on either side of the mask. Thread a pipe-cleaner through each hole and twist the end to hold it in place. To wear the mask, hook the pipe-cleaners around your ears.

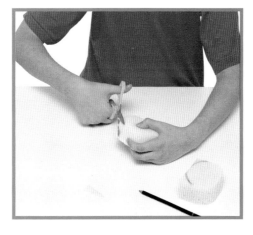

2 To make the rabbit's cheeks, draw a large circle on both bath sponges and cut them out. Make the circles as large as possible, then trim them to fit.

4 Glue on the sponge cheeks using PVA glue. The sponge will absorb the glue, so apply lots. Allow plenty of time for the glue to dry. Ask an adult to cut the pointy ends off the skewers. Dab a little PVA glue on to one end of each of the skewers. Insert three skewers into each sponge for the whiskers. If the whiskers are too long, ask an adult to trim them.

Painting your mask

If you want to paint the rabbit's furry grey face you will need – black, white and red paints, a mixing palette, water pot, and fine and medium paintbrushes. It is best if you paint the mask before gluing on the cheeks, nose and teeth.

To help you get the colours and fur just right, refer to a photograph of a rabbit in a book or magazine.

To start, mix together black and white paint to make a pale grey colour. Use the medium paintbrush to paint the front of the mask, but do not paint the ears. Mix a little more black into the grey to make it darker. Use this colour to paint lots of short, fine lines radiating outward from the cheeks. While this dries, paint the ears pink. You can make pink by mixing white and red paint. Paint the edges of the ears grey. Paint lots of short, fine white lines, also radiating outward from the cheeks. When dry, finish making the mask.

Wicked Witch

Make yourself a naughty witch disguise to wear to a Halloween fancy dress party. To complete your awful transformation, make a broomstick from twigs and branches and wear a black cloak over your shoulders.

Handy hint

If you cannot find a plastic funnel to use for the witch's nose, form a cone from a piece of card.

To make a cone, cut out a circle 15cm (6in) wide. Cut the circle in half. Bend one half so that the straight edges overlap. Join the edges with tape. Trace around the base of cone on to the plate. Draw a slightly smaller circle inside the outline. Cut out the small circle. Make shorts snips up into the base of cone. Fold out these flaps and push the cone into the hole. Glue the flaps to the back of the plate.

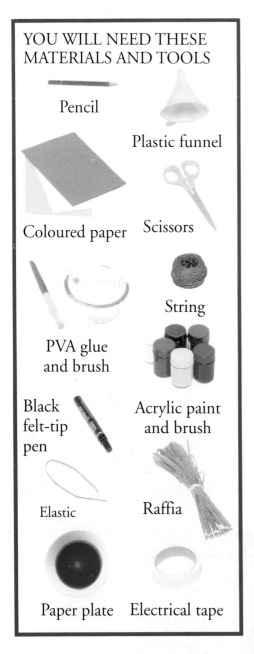

YOU WILL NEED THESE MATERIALS AND TOOLS

Pencil

Plastic funnel

Coloured paper

Scissors

PVA glue and brush

String

Black felt-tip pen

Acrylic paint and brush

Elastic

Raffia

Paper plate

Electrical tape

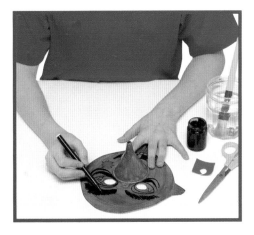

1 Draw a witch's face with a pointy chin on to the back of a paper plate and cut it out. Cut out holes for eyes. Place the funnel in the centre of the plate and trace around it. Cut out the circle, slightly inside the drawn line. Glue the funnel over the hole.

2 Mix a little PVA glue into green paint – the glue will help the paint stick to the funnel. Paint the face and funnel green. Cut out a small circle of red paper and glue it to one cheek to make a wart. Draw and colour in other features with a black felt-tip pen.

3 Undo the bundle of raffia and cut it into long lengths for the witch's hair. Tie the lengths of raffia together at one end with a piece of string. Use a piece of electrical tape to fix the bundle of raffia to the back of the plate.

4 Make a hole on each side of the mask. Thread a long length of elastic through one hole and tie it on. Put the mask on your face. Cut the elastic to the right length and knot it on to the other hole.

If this gruesome, green mask does not scare your friends and family, then nothing will. To really play the part of a witch, make up some spooky spells and carry around a pot full of plastic spiders and frogs!

147

Crazy Glasses

These glasses are inspired by the ones you find in joke shops. Crazy Glasses will really let you make a spectacle of yourself!

1 Draw a glasses shape on the black card. Use the pair of glasses as a guide for size and for the shape around your nose. You will need to use a light-coloured pencil or the outline will not show up. Cut around the outline.

2 Cut out two of the compartments from an egg box to make the eyes. Make a hole in the centre of each one for you to see through. Cut a piece of card from the lid of the egg box for the nose. Paint them and leave to dry.

3 When dry, glue the eyes and nose on to the frame of your Crazy Glasses with PVA glue. To make sure the nose is firmly fixed, use masking tape to hold it in position. While the glue is drying, prop up the nose with a pencil. Paint two pipe-cleaners black and leave to dry.

To finish, apply PVA glue to the ends of both arms of the Crazy Glasses. Wind a black pipe-cleaner several times around each glued area and leave to dry. Bend the pipe-cleaners round your ears to keep your crazy specs in place.

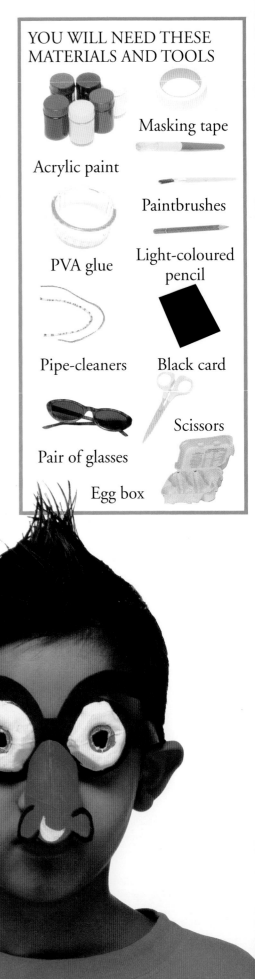

148

Fish Focals

Masks can be made using almost anything!
Here, a pair of swimming goggles is used
to make a very fishy mask.

Swimming goggles

Pencil

Masking tape

Glue stick

Coloured card

Black felt-tip pen

Scissors

Ruler

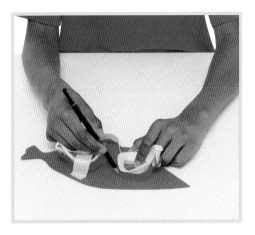

1 Draw a fish shape 25cm x 10cm
(10in x 4in) from card. Cut it out.
Place the swimming goggles on to the
fish and draw around the outline. To
make this easy, hold the goggles in
position with masking tape. Also cut
from different coloured card, a small
circle for the eye and fronds of seaweed.

2 Remove the goggles and cut out
the eye holes following the
lines you have drawn. Cut
four small vertical slits, two
on the outside edge of each
eye hole. Make sure the slits
are large enough to fit the
strap on the goggles.
Remove the strap from
your goggles.

*To finish, glue the eye on
to the fish and use a
felt-tip pen to
draw scales and
fins. Glue
fronds of
seaweed to
the mask.*

3 Push the swimming goggles into the
holes of the Fish Focals. If they do
not fit, make the eye holes on the mask
at little larger. Reattach the strap to the
goggles by threading the strap through
the slits in both goggles and the mask.

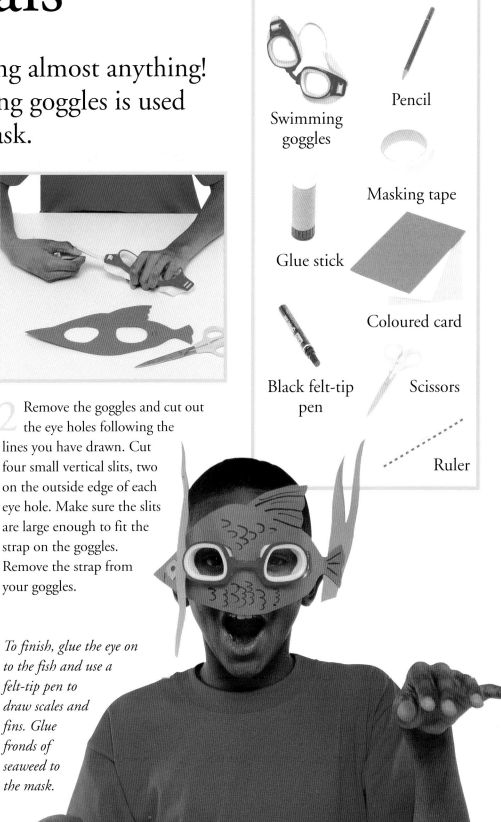

Hungry Wolf, Unlucky Lamb

This type of mask is called a transformation mask because it changes from one animal into another. It comes from the north-west coast of America. This mask tells the story of an unlucky lamb eaten by a wolf.

YOU WILL NEED THESE MATERIALS AND TOOLS

Two round foil baking trays

Plastic cup

Black felt-tip pen

Scissors

Acrylic paint and brush

PVA glue and brush

Glue stick

Pair of shoelaces

Wide electrical tape

Red, black and white paper

Elastic

'Watch out Lamb, the Hungry Wolf is about, and he cannot wait to gobble you up!'

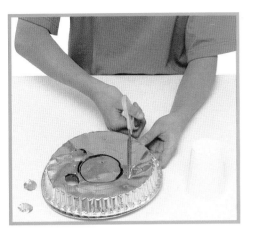

1 Place an upturned plastic cup into the centre of one of the baking trays. Draw around the cup with the black felt-tip pen. Remove the cup. Inside the circle, draw a hole for your nose. Then draw eye and mouth holes. Cut out the nose, eye and mouth holes.

2 Place the cut tray inside the other tray and trace around the nose, eye and mouth holes. Separate the trays and cut around the lines. Take the tray with the outline of the circle in the middle and cut it in half, straight down the middle between the eye holes.

3 Use PVA glue to stick the upturned plastic cup on to the back of one half of the halved tray. Position the cup on the felt-tip line. Do not worry if the glue spreads – PVA glue is invisible when dry. Allow plenty of time for the glue to dry thoroughly.

5 Place the two halves of the wolf mask on top of the lamb mask – the eye and mouth holes must line up. Use masking tape to hinge the wolf masks to the lamb mask. Open the mask and make hinges on the inside. Paint over any visible tape. Tape a shoelace to the bottom of each half of the wolf mask. Tie the laces to keep the mask closed. Make a small hole through both masks on each side. Try on the mask before cutting and tying on the elastic strap.

4 To paint foil, always add a little PVA glue to the paint colour before applying. Paint both halves of the halved tray red. Cut out red, black and white paper to make a pair of pointed ears, sharp white fangs and large oval eyes for the wolf. Paint the end of the cup black. Paint the other tray white. Use red and black paint to add the lamb's features. Paint a blue tear on the lamb's cheek. Allow the masks to dry.

To reveal the Unlucky Lamb mask, undo the shoelace tie at the front. The blue pieces of electrical tape show how the shoelaces are attached and where the hinges are placed.

Coco the Clown

If you enjoy the circus, then you will love this jolly mask. Use colourful or shiny pan scrubbers to make the clown's wild hair.

Handy hint

To make Coco's hair you can use copper- or silver-coloured pan scrubbers or brightly coloured plastic ones in yellow, green, purple, red or blue. Use different coloured pan scrubbers to make Coco's hair really wild! You can buy pan scrubbers in supermarkets or hardware shops.

YOU WILL NEED THESE MATERIALS AND TOOLS

Pencil

Two paper plates

Scissors

PVA glue and brush

Raffia

Acrylic paint and brush

Electrical tape

6 paper fasteners

6 pan scrubbers

Elastic

Small plastic lid

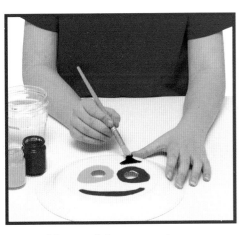

1 Hold one of the paper plates up to your face and ask an adult to mark eye holes. Cut out the eye holes. On the back of the plate, paint your clown face. Allow the paint to dry.

2 Draw a triangular hat and bow tie on the remaining paper plate. Cut them out. Paint and decorate the hat and bow tie with paint and coloured electrical tape. Finish the hat with a tassel of raffia. Attach the raffia with electrical tape.

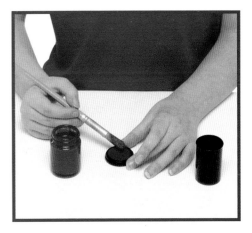

3 To make the clown's nose, use the plastic lid from a tube of sweets or plastic juice container. Mix a little PVA glue into some red paint and paint the nose. When dry, glue the nose on to the clown's face. Use PVA glue to stick on the hat and bow tie. Allow glue to dry.

4 Push a paper fastener through a pan scrubber and position it near the top edge of the plate. Push the paper fastener through the plate and flatten the fasteners. Attach the remaining pan scrubbers in the same way. Make a small hole in each side of the mask. Tie the elastic to one hole, then fit the mask before tying the elastic to the other hole.

Clown outfit

To make a clown outfit very quickly, attach colourful pan scrubbers down the front of a T-shirt and to the front of your shoes. Electrical tape is also great for jazzing up a pair of plain jogging pants. Use it to make stripes, checks and wacky patterns.

Bush Spirit Mask

The idea for this mask comes from the Pacific island of Papua New Guinea. It is made for ceremonies that celebrate the bush spirits, or Kovave. This card and fabric mask is a simple version of the real one. The fringe at the bottom of the mask covers the wearer's shoulders and gives the effect of a bird's body.

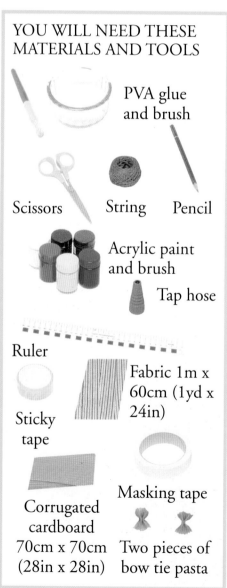

YOU WILL NEED THESE MATERIALS AND TOOLS

PVA glue and brush

Scissors   String   Pencil

Acrylic paint and brush

Tap hose

Ruler

Fabric 1m x 60cm (1yd x 24in)

Sticky tape

Masking tape

Corrugated cardboard 70cm x 70cm (28in x 28in)   Two pieces of bow tie pasta

Drape the strips of fabric over your shoulders and across your face. Then you can start to strut and move like a bird.

1 Fit the piece of cardboard around your head and fix the join with masking tape. The rippled side of the cardboard should be facing out.

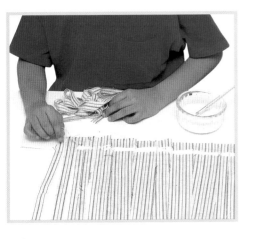

4 To make the fringe, cut the fabric into 2cm (3/4in) wide strips. Attach one end of the strips to a 70cm (28in) length of sticky tape. Overlap the strips. Glue the fringe inside the bottom edge of the mask.

5 Make a small hole on each side near the base of the mask. Knot a piece of string to each hole and tie under the chin.

2 Glue the cardboard at the join. Leave it to dry and remove the masking tape. Paint the tap hose brown, adding some PVA glue to the paint so that it sticks to the plastic. Paint brown stripes on to the cardboard. Paint between the stripes white.

3 When the paint on the tap hose is dry, fix it to the cardboard with PVA glue to make the bird's beak. Use plenty of glue and do not worry about spills – PVA glue is invisible when dry. Glue on pasta pieces for the eyes. Allow the glue to dry thoroughly.

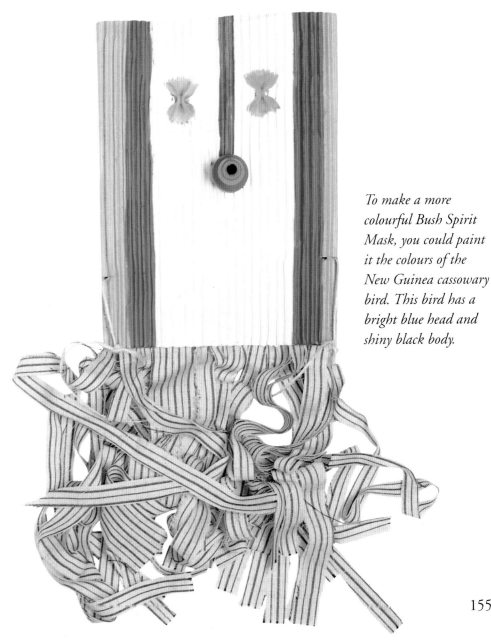

To make a more colourful Bush Spirit Mask, you could paint it the colours of the New Guinea cassowary bird. This bird has a bright blue head and shiny black body.

Beaky Bird

This mask has a beak that opens and closes. The idea comes from the ceremonial masks made by Native American Indians.

Papier-mâché

Papier-mâché involves gluing small squares or strips of newspaper on to a shape, mould, to make it stronger or to change its shape.

To make the glue, mix together equal quantities of PVA glue and water in a dish. Dip the newspaper pieces into the glue and smooth them on to the shape until it it covered.

Allow to dry before applying a second layer of papier-mâché.

YOU WILL NEED THESE MATERIALS AND TOOLS

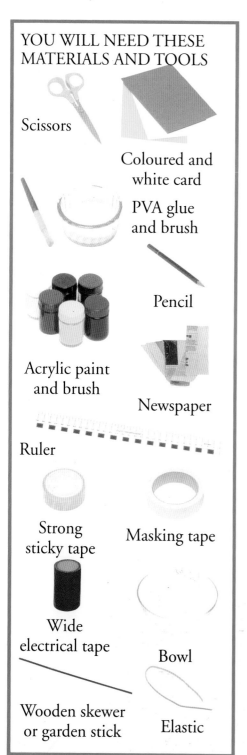

Scissors

Coloured and white card

PVA glue and brush

Pencil

Acrylic paint and brush

Newspaper

Ruler

Strong sticky tape

Masking tape

Wide electrical tape

Bowl

Wooden skewer or garden stick

Elastic

1 Draw on to card one lozenge shape for the face 30cm x 10cm (12in x 4in), two triangles for the upper beak 15cm x 3cm (6in x 1¼in) and two rectangles for the lower beak 15cm x 8cm (6in x 3in). Cut out all the pieces.

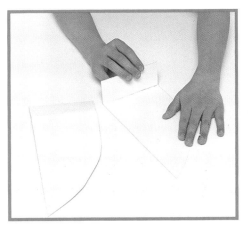

2 To make the beak, trim the two rectangles (for the lower beak) to match those shown above. Use scissors to score a fold line along the short edge of all four beak pieces. Bend each piece along the fold line to form a small flap.

3 Use masking tape to join the curved edge of the lower beak pieces. Take one of the upper beak triangles and tape its long edges to the long edges of the lower beak. Fold the flaps inward and tape over the hole. The shape should resemble the bow of a boat. Cover the beak with papier-mâché. When dry, tape the skewer to the front of the beak. Do two more layers of papier-mâché.

4 Glue the flap of the remaining upper beak piece on to the face. When dry, paint the face and beak.

5 Cut out a plume from card and glue it to the back of the mask. Hinge the bottom of the lower beak on to the mask with electrical tape.

To finish, make a small hole on both sides of the mask. Tie a length of elastic to each hole. When you are ready to make Beaky Bird squawk and talk, tie the elastic at the back of your head and use the skewer to move the lower beak up and down.

Talking House

Not all masks are of animals or humans. You can also create wonderful illusions using masks of inanimate, or non-living, objects. The Talking House mask is one of these very clever illusions. Once you have made the Talking House, see how many other objects you can turn into funny masks.

Handy hint

To create a really convincing illusion, make a costume to wear with your Talking House mask. If you dress in green and tape cotton wool bushes on to your T-shirt, your house will become the house on the hill. To create the illusion of a beautiful garden outside your house, wear a flowery shirt. Make a path to the front door with yellow electrical tape.

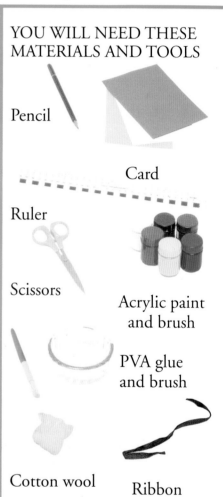

YOU WILL NEED THESE MATERIALS AND TOOLS

Pencil

Card

Ruler

Scissors

Acrylic paint and brush

PVA glue and brush

Cotton wool

Ribbon

If you and your friends all make Talking House masks, you would have the whole street talking!

1 Draw a house (with a smoking chimney) 25cm x 30cm (10in x 12in) on a piece of card. Draw in two eye holes and a hole for your nose.

2 Cut out the house shape. Cut out the holes for the eyes and the nose.

3 Paint the house red. When dry, paint rows of bricks and roof tiles in yellow. Paint window and door frames and the trunk of a tree black.

Add as many details to your house as you like. You could even make a Talking House that is exactly like your own house!

4 Tease some cotton wool to resemble billowing smoke and glue it to the chimney. Lightly dab the cotton wool with grey paint. Repeat to make the top of the tree, but lightly dab the cotton wool with green paint.

5 Make two holes just above the eye holes. Thread a long piece of ribbon through the holes, as shown.

Spotty Crocodile

There is a long tradition in mask-making of using everyday materials from around the home. With this crocodile mask, an ice-cube tray takes on a new life!

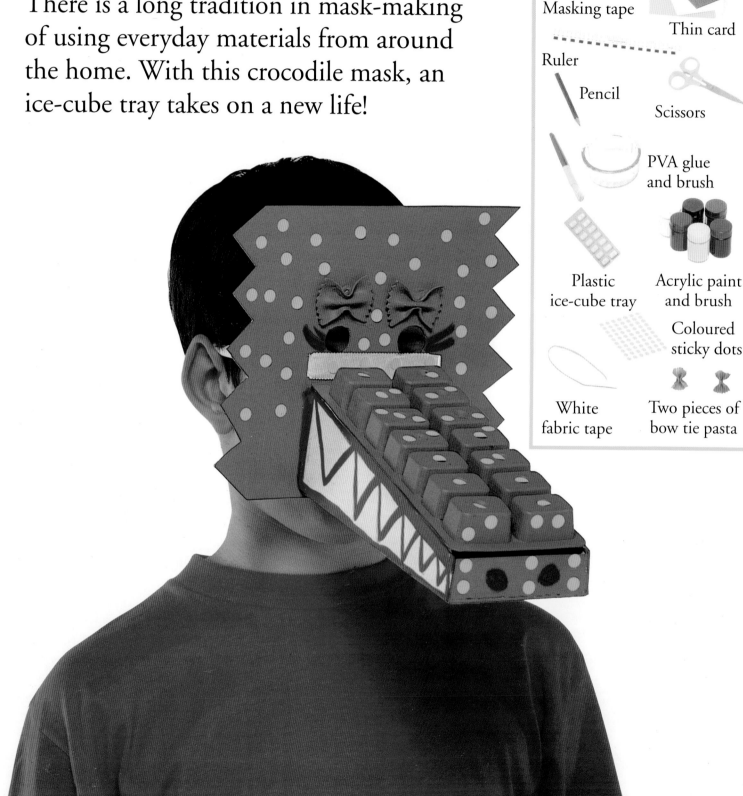

YOU WILL NEED THESE MATERIALS AND TOOLS

Masking tape

Thin card

Ruler

Pencil

Scissors

PVA glue and brush

Plastic ice-cube tray

Acrylic paint and brush

Coloured sticky dots

White fabric tape

Two pieces of bow tie pasta

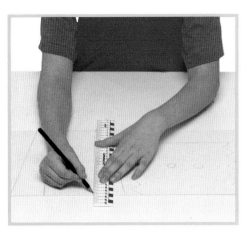

1 Draw a 20cm (8in) square on card. Draw eye holes, and a zigzag line down two edges. Do two tracings of the ice-cube tray on to card. Add tabs, the same depth as the tray, to every side of both tracings. Make the tabs on the long sides of one tracing, wider at one end.

2 Cut around the outlines and cut out the eyes. Make fold lines by scoring all lines on the snout with scissors. Make the lower jaw by folding and gluing the tabs together. When dry, glue the ice-cube tray on top of the snout. Use masking tape to keep things in position while the glue dries.

3 Glue the snout to the face. Carefully cut two slits in the face just above the snout, as shown. Glue pasta above the eyes. Paint Spotty Crocodile's face and the top and front of its snout blue. Paint the sides of the snout white and mark teeth in red. When dry, cover the crocodile with coloured sticky dots.

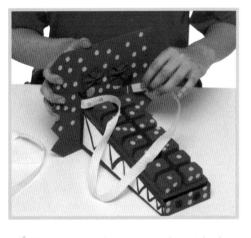

4 Thread the fabric tape through the slits, as shown. The tape will show, so decorate it with a line of sticky dots. Tie the tape around your head.

Animals with snouts

This method of creating a long snout using card, can be used to make other long-snouted animals like horses, giraffes or even dogs. To adapt this snout for other less-snappy creatures, simply make the rectangles shorter and the sides wider. You can add ears and horns by simply cutting them out of card and gluing them on to the face. Then all you have to do is paint and decorate your animal mask!

To make your crocodile mask look more realistic, find a photograph in a book and copy the colours. If you make two identical crocodile masks, you and a friend could play SNAP!

Spanish Giant

This mask is made to sit on top of your head. Nylon netting fabric falling from the mask covers your face. Masks like this one are used in Spanish carnivals and are often two or three times the size of a person.

Handy hint

When painting the face, make sure you leave enough space under the mouth so that the base can be trimmed. If you prefer, you could fit the mask and make holes for the elastic before you start painting.

To trim the mask, use scissors. If you find the papier-mâché too hard to cut, ask an adult to help.

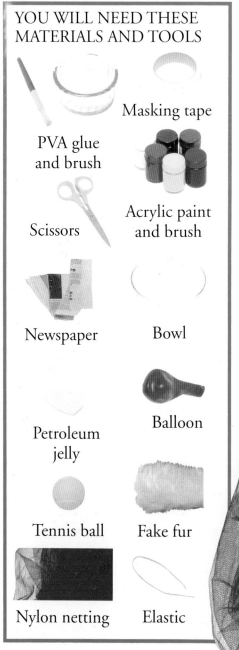

YOU WILL NEED THESE MATERIALS AND TOOLS

PVA glue and brush

Masking tape

Scissors

Acrylic paint and brush

Newspaper

Bowl

Petroleum jelly

Balloon

Tennis ball

Fake fur

Nylon netting

Elastic

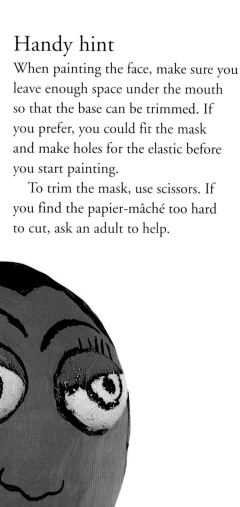

1 Inflate the balloon and tie a knot in the end. Cover the balloon with petroleum jelly. Make papier-mâché glue by mixing equal amounts of PVA glue and water. Glue strips of newspaper over the balloon to cover it. Do three layers.

2 Leave the papier-mâché somewhere warm to dry. When it is hard and thoroughly dry, deflate the balloon by snipping off the top of the balloon. Pull the balloon out of the papier-mâché shell and discard the balloon.

3 Ask an adult to help you cut an old tennis ball in half. Glue the halves on to the papier-mâché shell for the eyes. Use plenty of glue and hold the halved balls in place with masking tape while the glue dries.

4 Paint the mask. Use a thick brush to paint large areas and a thin brush to paint details. Some areas may need two coats. Allow to dry.

5 Trim the base of the mask so that it sits on your head. Make holes near the base of the mask. Attach elastic to one hole. Get a friend to hold the mask on your head while you fit the elastic strap under your chin. Pull on the elastic to get a snug fit, then tie the elastic to the hole.

Your own design

Design your own face for the Spanish Giant. It does not have to be a woman, it could be a scary monster, a funny clown or an alien. You could even paint your own face on to the mask!

6 Tape layers of nylon netting inside the base of the mask. Glue on a strip of fake fur to make a collar.

Face and Body Painting

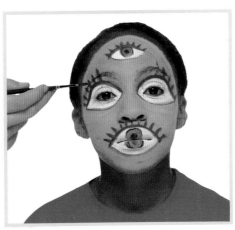

Thomasina Smith

Introduction

Face and body painting has a tradition that goes back thousands of years. In many ancient cultures, face and body painting was used to camouflage tribespeople when they went hunting. In other societies, face and body painting was an important part of religious ceremonies and cultural customs.

In our society today, we use face and body painting mostly to have fun and to entertain. You can face paint yourself for special occasions, fancy dress parties, school plays or to go to a wonderful street carnival. Even putting on ordinary make-up is a form of face painting.

When your friends see your Spotty Puppy face painting, they will all want it done!

Become anyone you want

Face painting can transform you into someone, or even something, entirely different. With little more than a collection of face paint colours, sponges and brushes you can become a Prowling Leopard, a Spotty Puppy, a Disco Diva or even a many-eyed alien.

Body painting

There is no reason for the face painting fun to stop at your neck. You can also paint your body and limbs using exactly the same materials. Watch your hands being transformed into a proud Stag, a very rare species of Octopus, a Little Devil and even a Digital Soccer star. Once you realize the possibilities and how easy it is to create some very funny characters, there will be no stopping you!

The only difference between face and body painting, is that body painting can take longer. So, be patient and try not to laugh when a ticklish spot is being painted.

You can paint just one hand or your whole body. This funny character is the very rare pentapus. It is an octopus with only five tentacles.

Someone to help

It is very difficult to do your own face and body painting. The best idea is to ask a patient friend or adult to help. You can always promise your make-up artist that you will paint their face or body in return.

Before you get out the face paints and brushes, read through the information on Basic Techniques on the following pages. This information will show you how to achieve stunning effects and a professional finish.

To give Super Robot's face a metal-like finish, it has been painted with silver face paint.

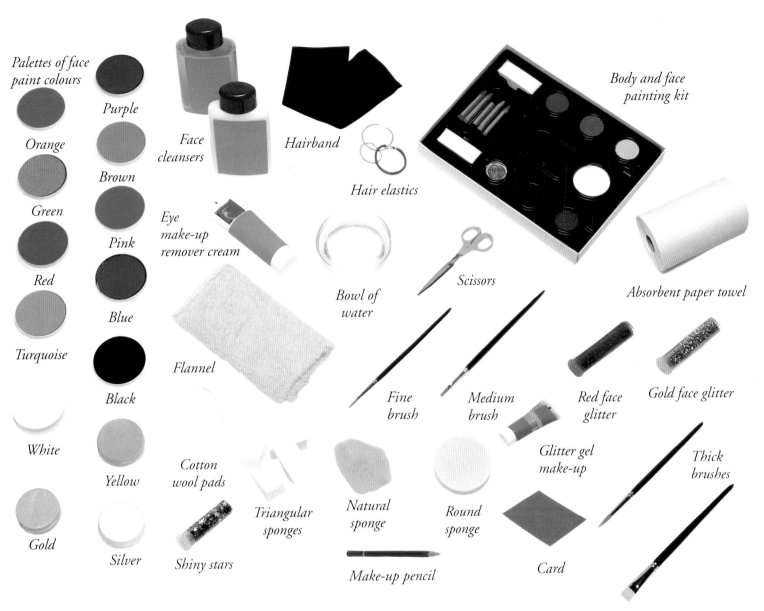

Palettes of face paint colours

Purple

Orange

Brown

Green

Pink

Red

Blue

Turquoise

Black

White

Yellow

Gold

Silver

Face cleansers

Hairband

Hair elastics

Eye make-up remover cream

Flannel

Cotton wool pads

Shiny stars

Triangular sponges

Bowl of water

Natural sponge

Scissors

Fine brush

Medium brush

Round sponge

Make-up pencil

Card

Body and face painting kit

Absorbent paper towel

Red face glitter

Gold face glitter

Glitter gel make-up

Thick brushes

Materials

Brushes You can buy special make-up brushes, or you can use good quality watercolour brushes. You will need three brushes to complete the projects in this book – a fine, a medium and a thick brush.

Face glitter This is specially made to be used on the face. It is available in speciality shops.

Face paints These are available in kits or in individual palettes. Buy professional face paints because they are easy to use, give a very good finish and are long-lasting.

Flannel and absorbent paper towel Use these for wiping away excess paints from your face.

Glitter gel make-up This is a clear, gel make-up that contains coloured glitter.

Make-up remover creams and cleansers These lotions will remove face paint without stinging. Always ask an adult before using any type of make-up removing product.

Natural sponge You can buy an inexpensive natural sponge in chemist shops and in some supermarkets. The texture of this sponge makes it ideal for creating a dappled effect.

Round sponge This smooth, round sponge is used for applying a base coat of face paint.

Shiny stars These tiny stars are made specially to be used on the face. They come in tubes and can be bought in theatrical shops. Stars can be glued to the face with special face glue.

Triangular sponges These are standard make-up sponges. It is a good idea to have two or three so that you do not have to wash them every time you change face paint colours.

Basic Techniques

Before you start, protect clothing with an old shirt or towel. It is a good idea if the make-up artist protects his or her clothing too. Cover the work surface with absorbent paper towels and lay out your materials. Always have a bowl of water handy.

Dip the brushes and sponges into water to dampen them before loading them with face paint. Always wash brushes when changing colours. When the water becomes discoloured, replace it with clean water.

How to apply the base colour

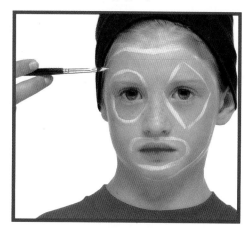

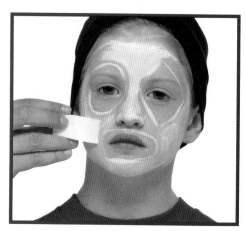

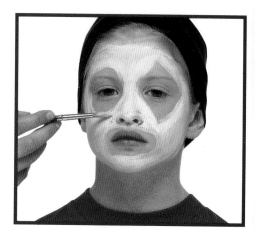

1 Use a medium or thick brush to paint the outline of a circle around the face and any other features. Paint the outlines in the base colour. The instructions will always state which colour should be used.

2 Dampen a round or triangular sponge in water. Rub the sponge gently around the face paint palette a few times to load sufficient colour on to the sponge. Fill in the outline with base colour.

3 When the outline is filled in, use a brush to neaten the edges. Use the sponge to get an even finish. In some cases, a second base coat will need to be applied to achieve this. Allow the face paint to dry between coats.

How to apply a two colour base

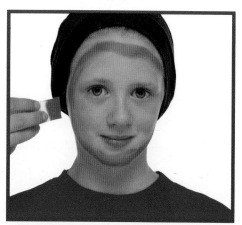

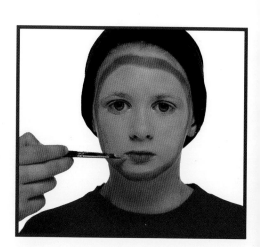

1 Outline the face using a triangular sponge or a round sponge folded in half. The instructions will always state which colour to use.

2 Use a clean sponge to apply the second colour. This colour will go inside the outline. To make the colours merge, go over with a damp sponge.

3 When the outline is filled in, use a fine or medium brush to neaten the edges. Use the brush also to touch up gaps around the nose, eyes and mouth.

Body painting

The technique for applying a base colour or second colour to the body or limbs is the same as for face painting.

Before starting body painting, put on the clothes you want to wear. Pulling clothes over the body painting may smudge it. Protect these clothes with an old shirt or towel. Always cover the work surface or floor with lots of absorbent paper towel or kitchen cloth.

Remember when wearing body paint that it will rub off on to furniture, clothes and anything you handle.

Removing make-up

Face and body paints can be easily washed off with mild soap and water. There is no need to rub hard.

Glitter gel make-up, face glitter, shiny stars and make-up glue are best removed using make-up remover creams and cleansers applied to cotton wool. Use special eye make-up remover cream to clean the sensitive skin around the eyes.

Always check with an adult before using any type of make-up remover, cleanser or cream.

Safety tips

It is a good idea to buy proper face paints. They will be more expensive than some alternatives, but they are easier to apply and therefore gentler on the skin. Some face paints are specially made for sensitive skins.

When you have finished face painting, gently rinse the surface of the palette under water. Wipe around the edge of the palette with a paper towel to remove excess face paint before replacing the lid.

If you do these things your face paints will remain clean, moist and ready to use.

Lay out a cloth. Apply the paint with a dampened sponge.

Allow the base to dry before applying the second colour.

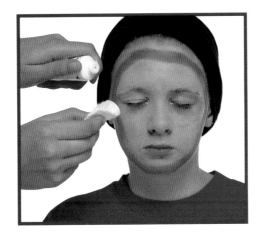

Close your eyes when face paint is being removed from around the eyes.

Dry your face and remove any traces of face paint with an old towel.

You must never use craft paints, felt-tip pens, crayons, craft glues or other stationery items on your face. They may cause an irritation.

Try not to accidentally touch wet face paint as it will cause the paint to smudge. Even when dry, face paint will smudge if it is rubbed.

Sea World

Would you like to be transformed into a living marine fantasy? It is easy and lots of fun. The crab painted around your mouth will twitch every time you smile or talk. When you blink your eye, the fish will look as though it is moving.

Handy hint

It is a good idea to wear an old towel around your neck and shoulders while your face is being painted. The towel will protect your clothes. It also provides your make-up artist with a handy place to wipe paint smudges from his or her hands and fingers.

Do not use a good towel – some dark face paints may leave a faint mark.

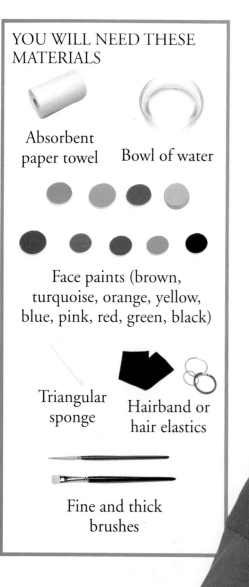

YOU WILL NEED THESE MATERIALS

Absorbent paper towel   Bowl of water

Face paints (brown, turquoise, orange, yellow, blue, pink, red, green, black)

Triangular sponge   Hairband or hair elastics

Fine and thick brushes

1 Tie the hair back. Paint a brown outline of a fish around one eye and on one cheek. Do this with the fine brush. Paint a turquoise circle around the face. Fill the circle using the sponge.

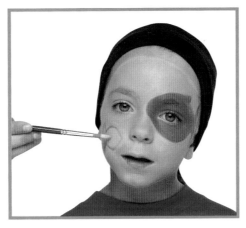

2 When the turquoise face paint is thoroughly dry, use the thick brush to paint one fish a glowing orange colour and the other a bright yellow. Allow to dry.

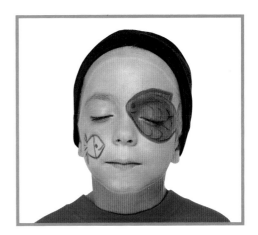

3 Paint the eyes, mouth, scales and fins on to the fish, using blue face paint and a fine brush. You must sit as still as possible while this is being done as it is quite fiddly!

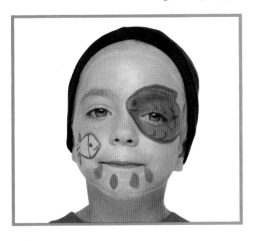

4 Break into a smile while your lips are being painted pink. Paint four pink crab claws just below the lower lip. The fine brush works best for detail work like this.

5 Use blue paint and a clean fine brush to outline and decorate the claws. Paint the face of the crab on the lower lip and draw in the stalks. Paint the crab's eyes red.

6 Use the fine brush to paint wavy green fronds of seaweed on to the forehead. To make the seaweed stand out, outline it in black face paint.

Underwater outfit to match

There is no need to spend money or lots of time making an outfit to go with your face painting. All you really need are sea-blue T-shirt and leggings, sheets of card, felt-tip pens, scissors, double-sided sticky tape and your imagination!

Draw some fishy, underwater-type creatures or vegetation on to card with the felt-tips pens. These drawings can be as large or as small as you like as long as they will fit on your T-shirt. Cut out the shapes. Press a piece of double-sided sticky tape to the back of each shape. Peel off the protective backing and press the shape on to your T-shirt.

Here are some ideas to get you started – tropical fish with trailing fins, a pod of dolphins, corals, shells and seaweeds. You could even include a pirate's treasure chest. When your Sea World fantasy is over, simply peel the pieces of card off your T-shirt.

Super Robot

This robot has supernatural abilities. Its radar vision can detect when enemy craft are approaching. The reflective metal helmet protects the robot during intergalactic battles. To make the helmet, cover a large, empty cereal box with aluminium foil.

YOU WILL NEED THESE MATERIALS

Round sponge

Hairband or hair elastics

Absorbent paper towel

Bowl of water

Fine and medium brushes

   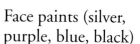

Face paints (silver, purple, blue, black)

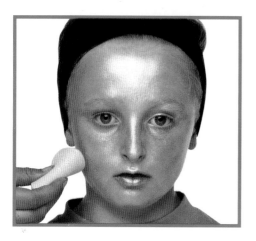

1 Tie the hair back. Close your eyes and mouth while your face is painted with the silver face paint using the round sponge. To make the silver stand out, apply two coats. Allow to dry.

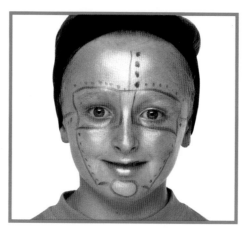

2 Use the fine brush to paint purple lines on to the face, as shown. Paint small purple dots beside the lines using the tip of the fine brush. This is the robot's reflective metal casing.

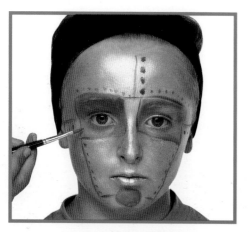

3 Paint the circle below the mouth with blue face paint using the medium brush. Then fill in the outlines around the eyes with blue face paint.

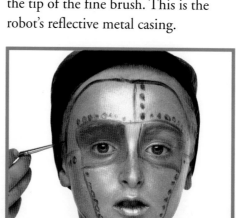

4 Wash the fine brush. Use the fine brush to paint a black outline around the face and to add more detail.

Pirate Peta

Welcome aboard landlubbers and meet one of the nastiest villains that ever sailed the high seas. This pesky, painted pirate has a black eye patch, curly moustache, pointy goatee and Jolly Roger tattoo. Peta's nose is pink because she does not wear sunblock.

YOU WILL NEED THESE MATERIALS

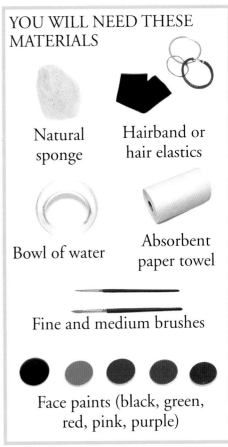

Natural sponge

Hairband or hair elastics

Bowl of water

Absorbent paper towel

Fine and medium brushes

Face paints (black, green, red, pink, purple)

A costume for Pirate Peta is easy to put together. All you need is a plain or striped T-shirt, a pair of baggy trousers, a sword, a rope and a head scarf.

1 Tie the hair back. Use black face paint and the fine brush to paint the moustache. It is a good idea to start at the centre of the lip and work outwards. Stay still while this is being done.

2 Paint the outline for the eye patch with the fine brush. Close your eye while the outline is filled with black. Paint a bushy eyebrow. Then paint the green straps for the eye patch.

3 Paint the skull and crossbones tattoo with red face paint and the fine brush. Use the medium brush to paint the pointy, black goatee.

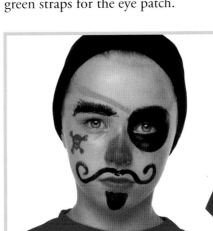

4 Use the natural sponge to dab the nose with pink face paint. Then dab purple face paint over the top of the pink.

Halloween Witch

Witches are an essential part of the Halloween tradition. This witch is a horrible shade of green – perhaps she ate someone nasty! She has a wrinkled face and lots of hairy warts. No wonder she does not look happy! To feel right at home in the role of a witch, why not make a broomstick from long twigs and have a spider for a pet?

YOU WILL NEED THESE MATERIALS

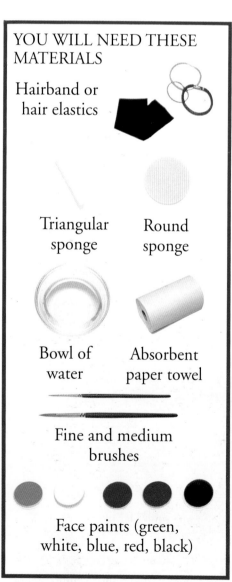

Hairband or hair elastics

Triangular sponge

Round sponge

Bowl of water

Absorbent paper towel

Fine and medium brushes

Face paints (green, white, blue, red, black)

Halloween Witch is wearing a black T-shirt draped with strands of purple raffia. Spiders and other creepy things cling to her clothes and hair.

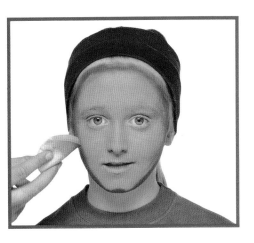

1 Tie the hair back. Use the triangular sponge to make a purple outline around the face. Fill the outline with green face paint using the round sponge. Blend the colours with the round sponge.

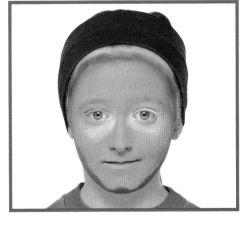

2 Before the green face paint dries, use the medium brush to paint above and below the eyes with white face paint. Dab this on quickly with the round sponge so that it will mix with the base colour.

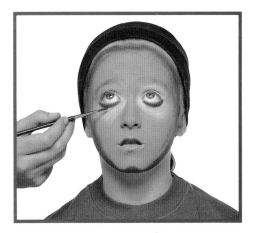

3 Mix white and blue face paints to make light blue. Paint the lower lip light blue using the medium brush. Look up towards the ceiling and keep your head still while a red line is painted under both eyes.

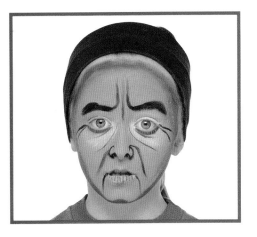

4 Paint black bushy eyebrows and wrinkles. Paint creases on the lips. Witches rarely smile, which is why they have deep frown lines.

5 Use the tip of the fine brush to paint red circles on the chin and forehead. Clean the fine brush before outlining the circles in black. Keep using the fine brush to paint black hairs sprouting from the warts.

Bind together lots of twigs and branches to make a broom. Halloween Witch needs a broomstick for getting about and for sweeping up around the cauldron!

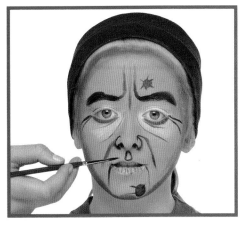

6 Use the fine brush and black face paint to accentuate the lines under the nose and add other gruesome features.

Spotty Puppy

There is only one thing more adorable than a puppy... a spotty puppy. The face painting for this extra cute canine is easy to do. It is perfect for someone trying their hand at face painting for the very first time.

If Spotty Puppy is going to a fancy dress party, she had better behave. No jumping on the furniture or chewing everything in sight!

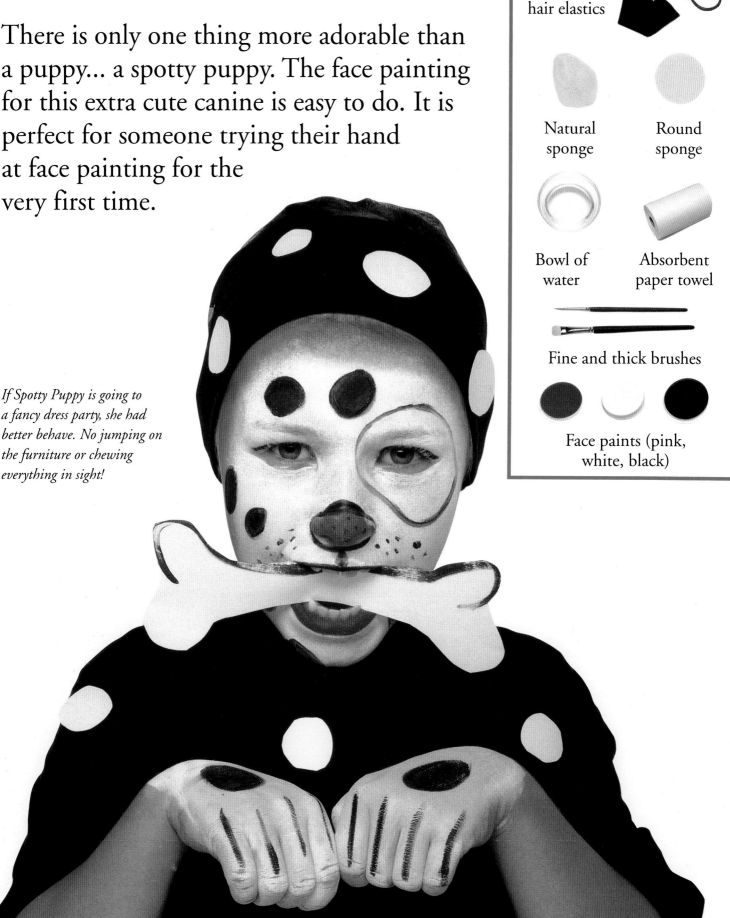

YOU WILL NEED THESE MATERIALS

Hairband or hair elastics

Natural sponge

Round sponge

Bowl of water

Absorbent paper towel

Fine and thick brushes

Face paints (pink, white, black)

1 Tie hair off the face. Use a thick brush to paint a thick pink circle around the edge of the face. Close your eyes and mouth while your face is being painted white with the round sponge. Do two coats if necessary.

2 Use the fine brush to paint a black circle around one eye and around the nose. Paint a black line from the base of the nose to the upper lip. Paint two black lines from the corners of the mouth to the jawline.

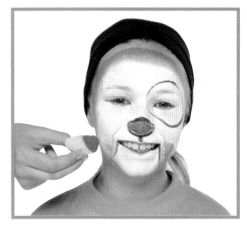

3 Colour the nose pink using the thick brush. Paint black dots on the nose with the fine brush. Dab pink face paint on either side of the mouth with a natural sponge. The sponge will create a dappled effect.

4 Make a smile while your lips are being painted. Use the fine brush to paint the upper lip black. Then paint the lower lip red.

5 Use the fine brush to paint black dots on to the cheeks. Paint circles on to the forehead, cheeks and chin with the fine brush. Paint the circles black. Close your eyes while a line is painted on to both eyelids.

To make the outfit, cut out circles of paper and stick them to a T-shirt and headband with double-sided sticky tape. Instead of painting your hands, you could wear socks covered with paper spots on your hands.

6 Paint the back of the hands white using the round sponge. Paint black lines on the fingers and four circles.

Octopus

This is a very rare and unusual species of octopus because it only has five tentacles instead of eight. Perhaps it should be called a pentapus – 'penta' meaning five. If you let pentapus get wet, he will disappear!

YOU WILL NEED THESE MATERIALS

Kitchen cloth   Bowl of water

Triangular sponge   Face paints (blue, red, black, white)

Medium brush

1 Lay a kitchen cloth on your work surface. Apply blue face paint to your hand with the triangular sponge. Leave to dry for a few minutes, then apply another coat with the medium brush. Leave to dry.

2 Turn your hand over and paint the palm pink. To make a strong pink colour, mix red and white face paints. Apply the pink using the sponge. Apply a second coat with the medium brush.

3 With the medium brush, paint white dots on your fingers. Leave to dry for a few minutes. Outline the white dots (suckers) with a fine line of black face paint.

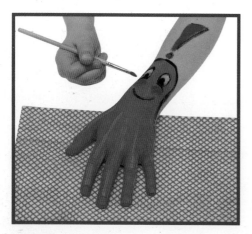

4 When the paint is dry, turn over your hand and paint the face of the octopus on to the blue background. Paint red lines down the fingers and an exclamation symbol (!) above the head.

Make a mini-stage for Octopus to perform in by decorating an empty cardboard box with paint and paper. You will need to leave the top of the box open so that you can put your hand on to the stage. Cut the front of the box to resemble draped stage curtains.

Stag

This painted hand puppet captures the elegant beauty of a proud stag. The antlers are formed using the little finger and first finger. Pinch together the two middle fingers and thumb to make the head.

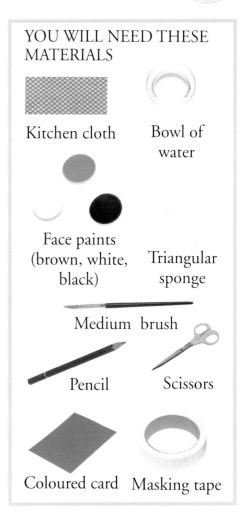
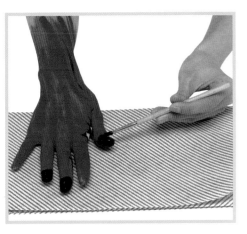

1   Rest your hand on a kitchen cloth. Apply brown face paint with the sponge. Leave to dry. Use the brush to apply streaks of light brown face paint. Paint the ends of your thumb and two middle fingers black.

2   Pinch your fingers together to make the stag's head and antlers. Paint the the eye white, as shown. Outline the eye with black and paint eyelashes.

To finish, draw two antlers on to card. At the base of each antler draw a narrow strip 5cm (2in) long. Cut the antlers out. Wrap the strips around your fingers and tape the ends.

3   Cut out a 2cm (³/₄in) circle of blue card to complete the eye. Paint a black dot in the middle. Tape the eye on to your middle finger using masking tape, as shown. Paint over the tape.

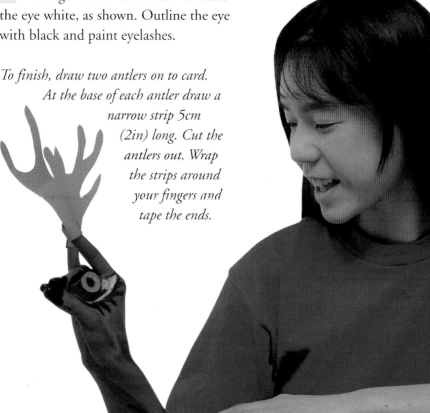

Flowering Tree

This body painting of a tree is so realistic you could almost hide undetected in a tropical jungle. Even the flowers winding their way up the trunk are exotic looking. If you moved your arms as though they were branches swaying in the wind, your camouflage would be complete.

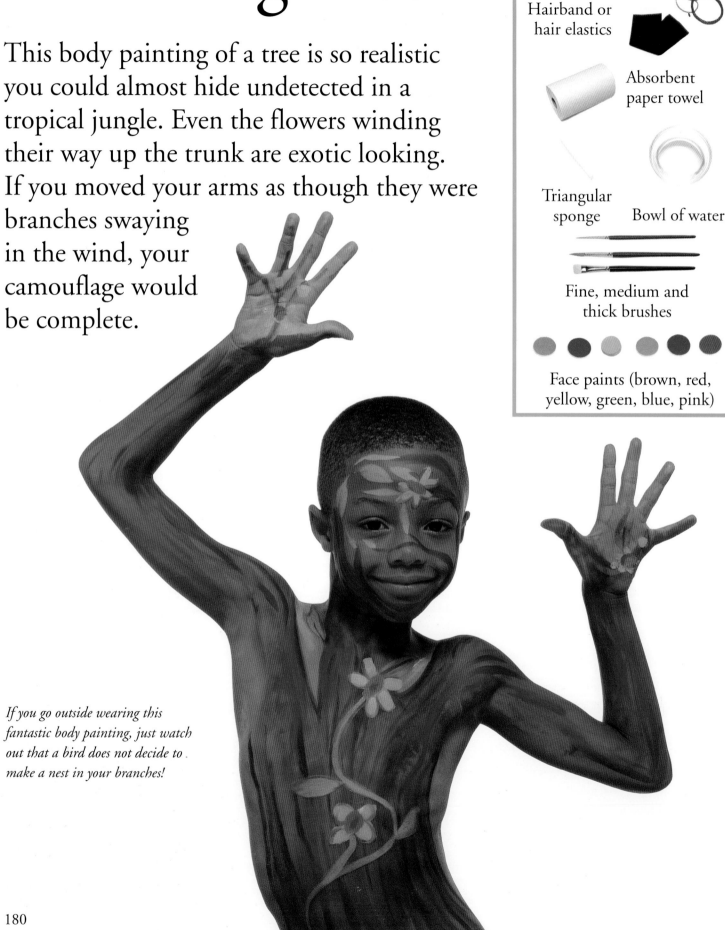

If you go outside wearing this fantastic body painting, just watch out that a bird does not decide to make a nest in your branches!

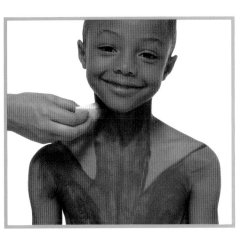

1 Tie the hair back. Use the medium brush to paint the brown outline of the tree trunk on to the chest and back. Use the sponge to fill in with brown face paint. Make shades of brown by adding red or yellow to brown.

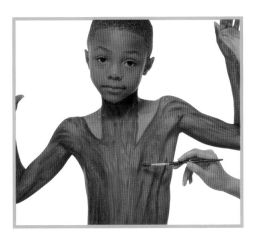

2 Paint the front and the back of the arms (the branches) in the same way. Extend the paint on to the hands but taper it to resemble the end of a branch. Do the texture of the bark using dark brown face paint.

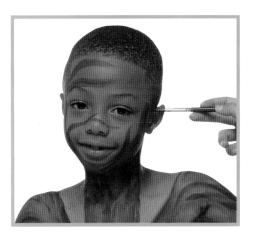

3 Use the thick brush and brown face paint to paint branches up the neck and on to the face. Make the branches twist and turn. Allow the paint to dry thoroughly before starting the next step.

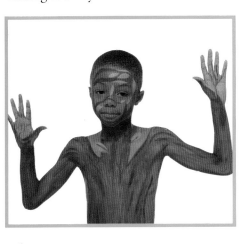

4 Wash the brush and sponge. Squeeze the sponge to get rid of excess water. Draw outlines for the leaves in green face paint. Fill in the outlines using the thick brush.

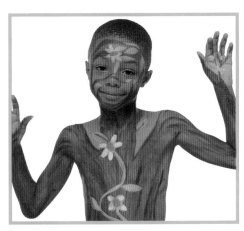

5 Paint a green stem spiralling up the trunk and linking all the leaves. Paint the flowers blue using a thick brush. Do two coats. When dry, paint the centres pink.

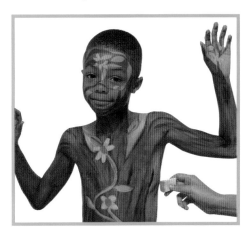

6 Use the clean sponge to paint in the background sky. This means filling in the unpainted areas with blue face paint. Apply it unevenly to look like a cloudy sky.

Making face paints go further

When you are painting a large area, like a person's body, with face paints always apply the paints with a triangular, round or natural sponge. Before dipping the sponge into the paint, dampen it in a little water. This will make the face paint go on easier and also make it go further. To even out face paint, dampen the sponge and wipe it gently over the area where the colour is concentrated.

You can mix face paint colours just as you would ordinary acrylic or poster paints. If you only need a little amount of a mixed colour, do the mixing on the lid of the palette. For large amounts of a mixed colour, use a smooth plate. To add sparkle to your face paint colours, mix in glitter gel make-up, face glitter or sequins.

181

Disco Diva

To dazzle all the other dancers at the disco, add a sparkle or two to your face with glitter gel make-up. It comes in lots of colours, so choose your favourites. Glitter gel make-up is easy to use, but it can be a little messy.

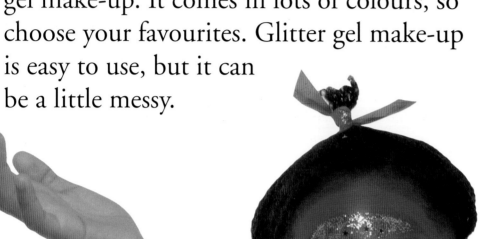

A diva is someone who is excellent at doing something. A Disco Diva is someone who knows all the dance moves and how to make them!

182

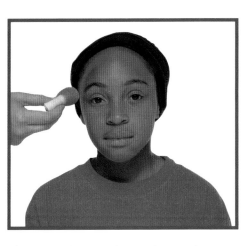

1 Tie the hair back. Apply a wide circle of pink face paint around the edge of the face using a damp round sponge. Do not worry if the circle is not perfect – the edges can be neatened with the fine brush.

2 Paint a turquoise line with the fine brush from the inside corner of each eye up to the end of each eyebrow. Fill in with turquoise using the thick brush. Blend in the colour with a damp natural sponge.

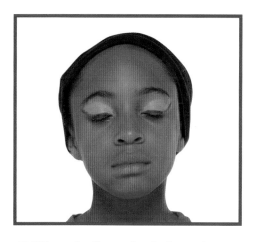

3 When the face paint is dry, paint two thin black lines on to the eyelids, as shown. Start the line from the inside corner of each eye and move outwards. Keep your eyes closed until the paint has dried.

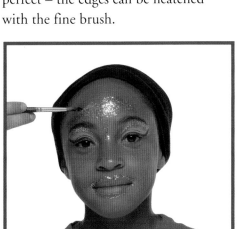

4 Use the glitter gel brush to paint the gold glitter gel on to the forehead, nose, eyelids and around the mouth. Glitter gel make-up is quite runny so apply it sparingly and carefully. When dry, apply another coat if necessary.

5 While the glitter gel is wet, gently press some stars on to the forehead and nose. Do not put lots of stars in one place, they will fall off. If the gel dries before the stars are in place, apply some more gel.

Sparkling extras

This would be a great time to spray your hair with a glitter hair spray. To remove the sparkling dust, rinse or brush your hair. You can buy glitter hair spray in specialist theatrical shops and some chemist shops.

6 Stretch your lips into a broad smile while bright pink face paint is applied to your lips with the thick brush. You have every reason to smile, Disco Diva, because you are ready to go dancing!

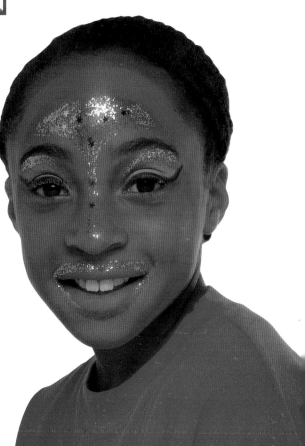

Prowling Leopard

Face painting is a great way to be transformed into an animal, especially an exotic jungle creature like this sleek, spotted leopard. To make your face look lean, mean and hungry, the outline around the face is a special shape.

YOU WILL NEED THESE MATERIALS

Hairband or hair elastics

Bowl of water

Absorbent paper towel

Face paints (yellow, orange, black, red, brown)

Fine, medium and thick brushes

Round sponge

Handy hint

If you use face paint on your hands, do not forget to keep your hands away from water. Even small splashes of water will wash away face paint.

184

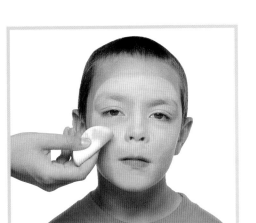

1 Tie the hair back. Paint a yellow circle around the face with a medium brush. Fill in the circle with yellow face paint applied with a round sponge. Try to apply the face paint smoothly and evenly.

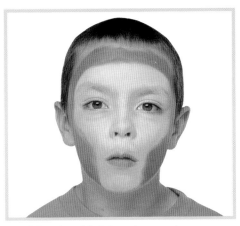

2 Use the thick brush to paint an outline around the face in orange face paint. Shape the outline, as shown. Neaten the edges with the fine or medium brush. Allow the base colour to dry thoroughly before continuing.

3 Close your eyes while black lines are painted on your eyelids. A fine brush will be needed for this. Paint the nose and the upper lip with black face paint. Paint the line that runs from the upper lip to the nose.

4 Even leopards can raise a smile so that their lower lip can be painted bright red. A fine brush will be needed to paint the lips.

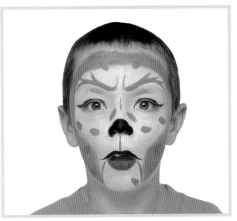

5 Use the fine brush to paint the sweeping eyebrows, spots and lines on the face brown. Try to do this as neatly as possible.

6 Paint tiny brown dots below the nose with the fine brush. Paint lines from these dots to make the leopard's whiskers. Growl!

Look out, leopard about!

To make yourself a really convincing leopard takes a little more than just face paint. You will have to prowl like a leopard – silently – and growl like a leopard. It also helps if you dress like this sleek lord of the jungle.

To make the ears, cut two oval shapes from orange card. Fold along the bottom to form a flap. Draw a line in felt-tip pen on each ear, as shown. Apply special make-up glue to the base of the flaps and press them on to your forehead. Adding spots to an orange T-shirt (and even jogging pants or leggings) is easy. Simply cut yellow circles from card and use double-sided sticky tape to attach them to the front and back of the T-shirt.

You can either paint the paws using face paint or wear a pair of gloves or socks on your hands. You can decorate the gloves or socks with circles and strips of card. Attach the card with double-sided sticky tape.

Fake Tattoo

A tattoo is simple to do when it is done with face paint. Better still, it will wash off with soap and water. Tattoos can be painted anywhere on your body. This tattoo consists of a banner, a heart and your initials.

YOU WILL NEED THESE MATERIALS

Bowl of water

Absorbent paper towel

Face paints (purple or black, red, green)

Fine and thick brushes

1 Paint the outline of the tattoo in purple or black using the fine brush.

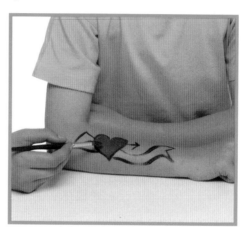

2 Allow the outline to dry before painting the heart red. Do this with the thick brush.

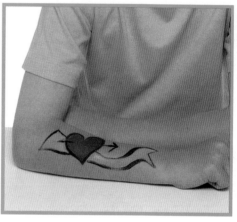

3 Clean the thick brush before using it to paint the banner green. Do two coats, if necessary.

Be more adventurous and artistic with your tattoo by including images of animals, flowers, cars, ships or even your favourite pair of roller skates.

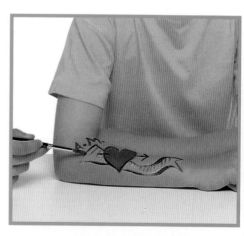

4 Paint the initials in purple or black face paint using the fine brush. Clean the fine brush. Decorate the banner with thin red stripes using the fine brush.

Jewels Galore

Use face paints to create fantastic jewellery. Do it for fun or to jazz up a fancy dress costume. Imagine how amazed your friends will be when you turn up at a party dripping with diamonds, rubies and sapphires!

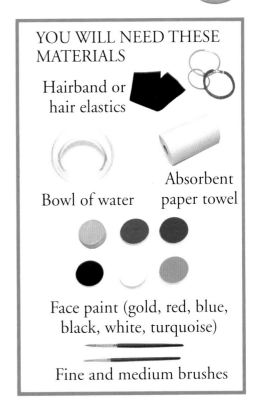

YOU WILL NEED THESE MATERIALS

Hairband or hair elastics

Bowl of water

Absorbent paper towel

Face paint (gold, red, blue, black, white, turquoise)

Fine and medium brushes

Handy hint

Gold face paint is a bit more expensive than other colours. If you do not have gold face paint, use yellow instead.

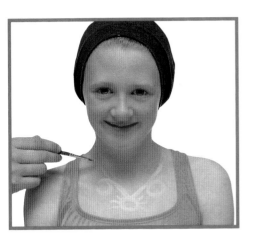

1 Tie the hair back. Paint the outlines of the necklace in gold face paint using a medium brush. Do two coats, if necessary.

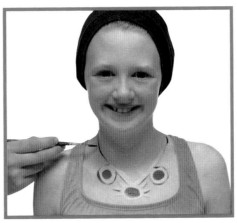

2 Fill in the outlines with red and blue face paints. Paint a thin black line around the necklace and pendants with a fine brush.

3 Paint a gold band around the wrist, then paint the outline for the watch face and straps black. Use the fine brush to paint the watch face white and the clock hands turquoise.

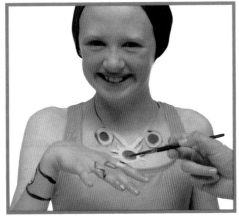

4 Use a clean fine brush to paint the gold outlines of rings on to the fingers. Allow to dry before painting exquisite turquoise, ruby and sapphire gems on to the rings.

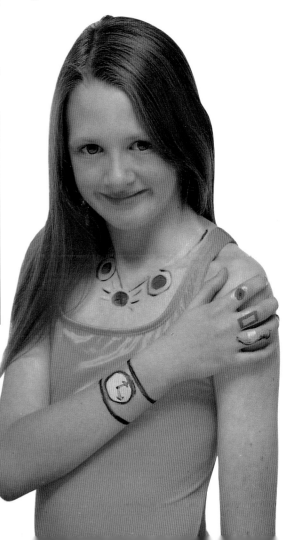

Football Hero

You do not have to buy your football team's strip – you can paint it on! Body painting is lots of fun especially when the paint is being applied to ticklish spots! Try not to laugh too much or you will end up with socks covered with wiggly lines. Remove body paint under the shower and dry yourself with an old towel.

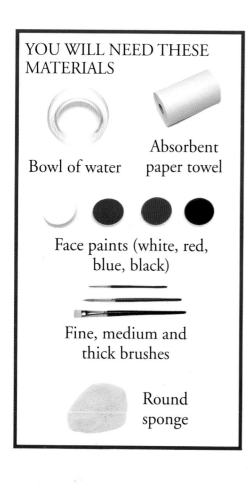

YOU WILL NEED THESE MATERIALS

Bowl of water

Absorbent paper towel

Face paints (white, red, blue, black)

Fine, medium and thick brushes

Round sponge

When painting the feet, apply paint only to the tops and sides. Black footprints all over the carpet might not be appreciated!

188

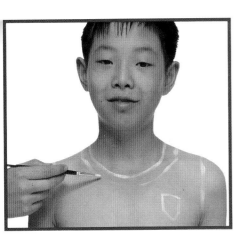

1 Make an outline on the chest and back in white face paint of the front and the back of the football shirt. This is best done with a medium or thick brush. Do not forget to paint the outline of the team's badge.

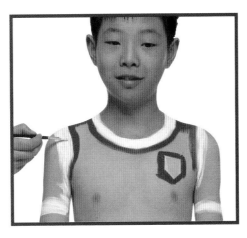

2 Use the thick brush to paint broad red lines inside the white outlines. Paint a red line around the waist. In white face paint, go over the outline to make the collar. Paint the sleeves white with a thick brush.

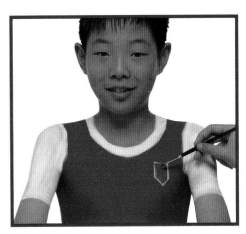

3 Use the round sponge to paint the rest of the shirt. To make the face paint go on easily, slightly moisten the sponge before applying the face paint. Paint the details on the badge using a fine brush.

4 Wash the sponge thoroughly and cover the floor with absorbent paper towel. Paint the tops of the feet black using the clean sponge. Use a thick brush to paint red and white bands around both legs.

5 Stand as still as you can while the black paint dries. When it is dry, paint on white boot laces with a medium or thick brush. To make the laces show up, apply the white face paint thickly.

6 Paint short black lines on to the top band with a medium brush. Then paint a black line around the leg for the sock turnovers. The paint must be dry before the football hero can hit the pitch and score the winning goal.

Digital Soccer

Get your friends together and paint each others hands in soccer strip. To play Digital Soccer, divide into two teams and move the ball around a tabletop pitch. Use your fingers to kick the ball into goal. Do headers by bouncing the ball off the back of your hands.

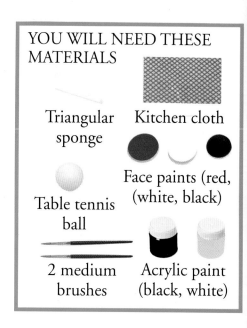

YOU WILL NEED THESE MATERIALS

Triangular sponge

Kitchen cloth

Table tennis ball

Face paints (red, (white, black)

2 medium brushes

Acrylic paint (black, white)

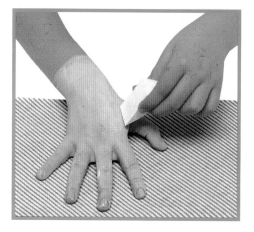

1 Lay the kitchen cloth on your work surface. Apply a base coat of white face paint to one or both hands with a triangular sponge. Leave to dry.

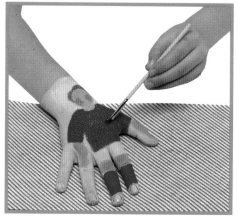

2 Paint the red socks and shirt with the medium brush. Paint the face, arms and knees in a skin tone colour. Leave to dry for a few minutes.

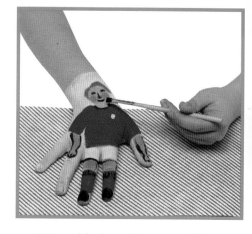

3 Paint a black outline around the footballer. Now you can paint in his black boots and facial features.

4 Paint a table tennis ball with black acrylic paint. When the paint has dried, carefully add the white markings you find on a football. World Cup Digital Soccer, here we come!

To make the pitch, cover a tabletop with newspaper or a large sheet of paper and use a felt-tip pen to mark the lines. Cut one long side end off two small boxes to make the goals. It does not matter what size the boxes are as long as they are exactly the same size. Fix the goals at either end of the pitch using double-sided sticky tape or sticky tack. You are now ready to kick off!

190

Little Devil

We can use our hands and fingers to make all sorts of shapes and creatures, including this Little Devil. Face paints, a cloak and a trident complete the illusion. The first and fourth fingers form the devil's horns. The two middle fingers curl over to make the hair.

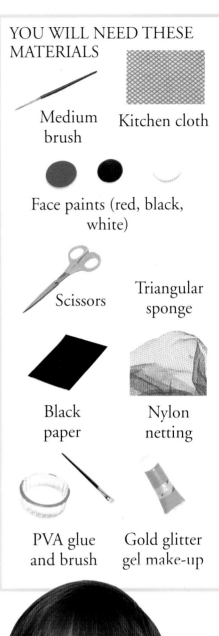

YOU WILL NEED THESE MATERIALS

Medium brush

Kitchen cloth

Face paints (red, black, white)

Scissors

Triangular sponge

Black paper

Nylon netting

PVA glue and brush

Gold glitter gel make-up

1 Lay down a kitchen cloth. Sponge the palm and back of the hand, wrist and thumb red. Paint the first finger and little finger white and the two middle fingers black with the brush.

2 When dry, paint the tip of the thumb and the base of the little finger black. Paint Devil's face and beard black using the medium brush. Outline the teeth with black and fill in with white face paint.

To finish, cut a length of red nylon netting and tie it around the wrist. Cut out a trident from black paper and glue it to the front of the cloak.

3 Use a finger to gently smear gold glitter gel make-up over the red paint on the wrist. This will make Little Devil's neck glint and shimmer.

Alien from Outer Space

Alien lifeforms can come in many different guises. This extra-terrestrial beauty is the famous many-eyed creature from the planet Agog. This alien sees everything. Even when asleep, the extra pair of eyes on its eyelids keep a watchful gaze. Just to be certain it misses nothing, there is a pair of cardboard eyes on straws attached to a headband. Double creepy!

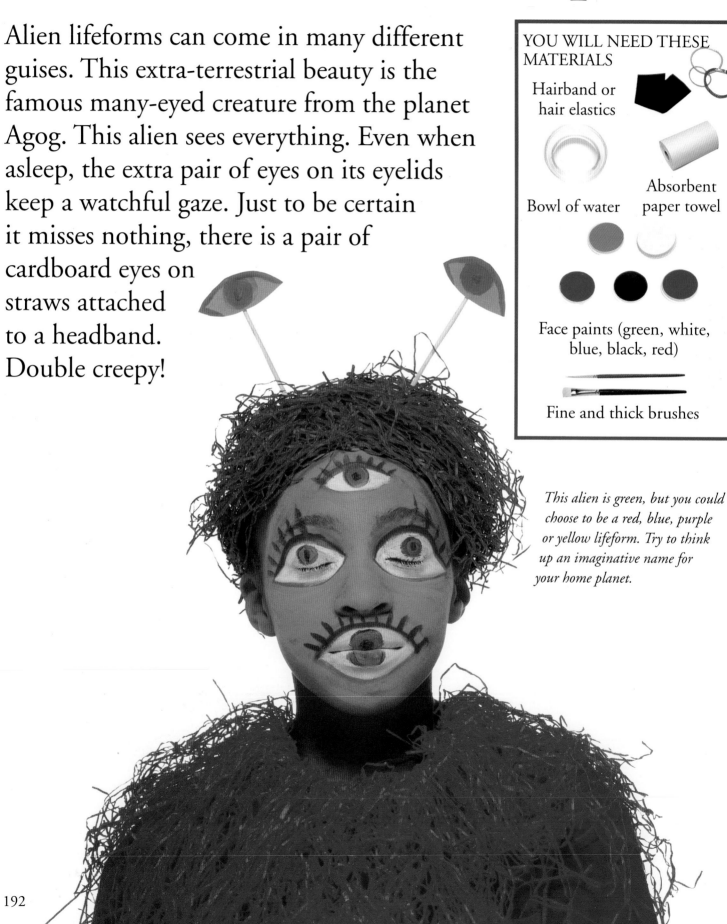

This alien is green, but you could choose to be a red, blue, purple or yellow lifeform. Try to think up an imaginative name for your home planet.

192

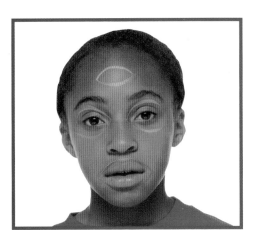

1 Tie the hair back. Use the fine brush to paint the outlines of four oval eye shapes in green face paint. You will need to close your eyes and mouth while the outlines are being painted.

2 Paint the outline of a circle around the face in green face paint with the thick brush. Do two coats, if necessary. Fill in the outline with green. Clean and dry the thick brush thoroughly.

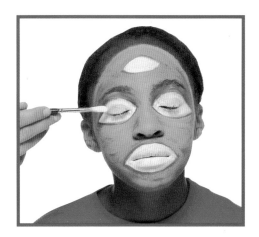

3 When the green face paint is dry, fill in the four eye shapes with white face paint. Do this with the clean thick brush. Apply the paint quite thickly and do two coats, if necessary.

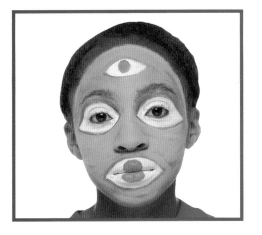

4 Allow the white face paint to dry thoroughly. Then paint blue circles on to the eyes on the lips and forehead. These are the irises of the eyes. Apply two coats if necessary.

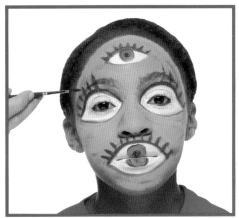

5 When the blue face paint is dry, paint a black dot on to the irises to make the pupils. Use the fine brush to paint a red line above the eyes and to make the eyelashes.

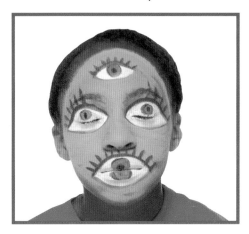

6 Close your eyes and stay very still while the irises are painted blue. When the paint is dry, paint on black pupils. Watch out! The many-eyed alien has arrived.

Alien costume

The planet Agog is covered with multi-coloured raffia and so are its inhabitants. Raffia is wound around their heads and used to form a cloak over their shoulders. But do you know what is under the cloak? More pairs of eyes, of course. When you make a pair of eyes to wear on your head, cut out and colour extra pairs and stick them to your T-shirt with double-sided sticky tape. When you open your raffia cloak to reveal the secret eyes, your friends will be agog!

To fasten the cardboard eyes to plastic straws, use sticky tape. To get them to stick on your head, bend the bottom of the straws and push them under a headband. If they wobble about, fix them to the headband with more sticky tape.

Clowning Around

Nick Huckleberry Beak

Introduction

So you want to throw things around and catch them again? Create animals out of thin air and rubber? Generally clown around and have fun? Well, you have come to the right place because this is all about juggling and crazy balloon modelling. But be warned – juggling fever is catching and balloon modelling can make your day go with a bang!

Juggling fun

Once you have learned the basics of juggling there is no turning back. You will start with balloon balls and bean bags, then you will want to juggle fruit, plates, cups, sneakers and small pieces of furniture. Before you know it you will be doing Under or Over juggling with the family pet, the Statue of Liberty and an elephant. Nothing is safe – everything can be juggled. Some of the juggling moves are really easy and you will catch on (ha! ha!) in a flash. Other juggling routines will take

This is how all new jugglers look – cross-eyed and confused!

practice, patience and a bit more practice. If you do not have juggling balls, do not worry – there are instructions for making your own balloon balls and bean bags. But if you just cannot wait to get juggling, you can practise with scarves, fruit (ask permission first) or even socks partially filled with uncooked rice. (Cooked rice is impossible to juggle with!) Do not try juggling priceless pieces of crockery or expensive electronic equipment – just yet!

Balloon modelling bug

Twist, twist, bend, bend, stretch, twist and pop! No, this is not a new dance, nor a new breakfast cereal. This is the sound of someone with the balloon modelling bug. The good thing about this bug is that it is fun to pass it on! Without so much as a huff or a puff, you will be able to create a world of hairless dogs, featherless birds and flowers that survive without water. You will even be able to build a light-filled, airy house with nothing more than 17 balloons and a balloon pump.

To start, you will make models for yourself, then you will perform feats of balloon magic at parties, fêtes and carnivals. But once the bug has really taken hold you will be balloon modelling while waiting for the bus, during school and under your duvet at night! It is not that you have gone mad, you have simply become a balloonatic!

This is the look of someone who has caught juggling fever and is having a great time!

This is a balloonatic. Her balloon modelling skills have gone totally to her head!

Materials

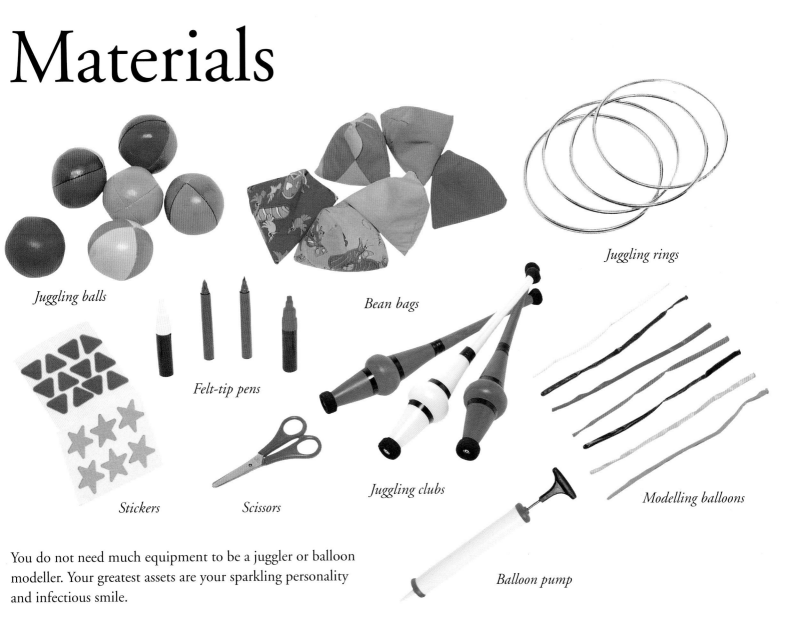

Juggling balls

Bean bags

Juggling rings

Felt-tip pens

Stickers

Scissors

Juggling clubs

Modelling balloons

Balloon pump

You do not need much equipment to be a juggler or balloon modeller. Your greatest assets are your sparkling personality and infectious smile.

Balloon pump There are many types of balloon pumps available, but you must make sure that you get one with a tapered nozzle on the end. These are specially made to inflate modelling balloons. The most effective type of pump is a double-action pump. This pump inflates the balloon when you push the pump in and when you pull it out.

Bean bags These are made from cotton fabric and shaped like pyramids. They are often filled with dried pulses. You can buy them in joke shops and theatrical supply shops, or you can make your own. You will need three or more bean bags.

Felt-tip pens To decorate and draw faces on to your balloon modelling creations you will need indelible felt-tip pens. Indelible means that your drawings will not rub off the smooth surface of the balloon.

Juggling balls These are soft, plastic-covered balls that come in lots of bright colours and patterns. You can buy inexpensive sets of juggling balls in toy shops and joke shops, or make your own using round, party balloons and uncooked rice.

Juggling clubs These can be bought in sets or separately, and they come in various sizes. They are quite expensive. In place of clubs, try your juggling moves with plastic skittles. You can even decorate the skittles to look just like the real thing.

Juggling rings When you become very confident at juggling, you could buy a set of juggling rings. They are made of metal and come in various sizes.

Modelling balloons These are long, thin balloons that come in a variety of colours. You can buy them in bags of 100 in toy and joke shops, and also in specialist theatrical suppliers. All the balloons used in these projects are the '260' type. Modelling balloons can lose some of their quality over time, and are best kept in a cool, dark place.

Scissors You will need a pair of scissors to cut balloons to make balloon balls, to make bean bags and to do one of the tricks.

Stickers You can use stickers to decorate balloon models and juggling equipment. Buy sheets of plain coloured or fancy stickers from toy shops and stationery shops.

Basic Techniques

Inflating modelling balloons and tying knots

Modelling balloons are easier to inflate and less likely to burst if they are warm. You can warm them by stretching them a few times and by keeping them out of the refrigerator. Do not leave balloons in sunlight – this will speed up the process of disintegration.

Bang! Some balloons are (pop! burst!) weaker than others. On average, about one in every 25 to 30 balloons bursts during inflating, so do not (bang!) worry – it is not your fault. Immediately discard the burst balloon and any small pieces that have fallen on the floor by putting them in the dustbin or out of reach of young children and pets.

The only trick to tying a knot in a modelling balloon is patience. If you take it slowly and keep a tight grip on the balloon, the balloon will be tied in knots, not you!

1 **Inflating the balloon** – carefully insert the nozzle of the pump into the mouth of the balloon for about 2cm (³/₄in). Hold the balloon in place. If you let go of the balloon while it is being inflated, you can easily imagine what happens.

2 Start inflating your balloon, but always leave an uninflated bit at the end. This is important as each time you twist the inflated balloon air will be forced down the balloon. The more twists used to create a model, the longer the uninflated end should be.

3 **Tying a knot** – this is often the cause of much frustration, but really it is not difficult. Hold the end of the mouth of the balloon tightly to keep it sealed. Then stretch the neck of the balloon around two fingers, as shown. Do not pull too tightly – it hurts. Ouch!

4 Pull on the end of the balloon until it crosses the neck of the balloon and the two fingers. Hold with the thumb.

5 Tuck the end of the balloon down between the two fingers and through the circle – in other words, tie a knot!

6 Keeping hold of the end, slip your fingers out of the knot and pull it tight. Phew!

Decorating your balloon models

You can make your balloon models more colourful, realistic or comical by drawing on them or decorating them.

The simplest and quickest way to decorate balloons is to use indelible felt-tip pens. As well as using a variety of bright colours, get hold of a white pen if possible. White is really effective when drawing eyes, as it makes them stand out.

Eyes, a nose and mouth are probably the first things you will want to give your animal balloon models. Why not also draw on paws, feathers or fur, or just wild and wonderful patterns? You could give Pampered Pooch, for example, a fancy collar and name tag. If you are making a model for a friend, you could write their name or a message on it. A balloon model elephant that says 'Happy Birthday' on one side would make a very unusual birthday card.

You can also use small stickers to decorate your models. Stickers come in lots of different shapes, textures and colours. There are even sticker packs of eyes, noses, ears and other facial features. Once your sticker is in position, you will not be able to remove it without bursting the balloon.

To apply paint to a balloon model, you first have to mix PVA glue into the paint before you apply it. The PVA glue will make the paint stick to the balloon. Apply the paint gently and use a soft brush.

Juggling safety tips

❖ Do not attempt to juggle with sharp or pointed utensils or heavy objects. Sharp things will cut you, and heavy objects will give you nasty bump on your head or will land slap, bang, ouch on your little toe!
❖ Make sure you have lots of room around you and above you when juggling. Ask an adult to move furniture out of the way so that you do not trip over. Breakable items should be moved to another country for safe keeping!

Just as well this girl was only juggling balloon balls!

Balloon modelling safety tips

Although we set out to have fun with balloons, they can be dangerous, so please follow these few simple precautions. Make sure your friends are also aware of these rules.

❖ Always keep uninflated or burst balloons away from young children and animals to prevent choking accidents.
❖ Never put a whole balloon or a piece of a balloon in your mouth.
❖ Keep balloons away from your eyes, especially when stretching or inflating them.
❖ Always use a balloon pump. Modelling balloons are very difficult to inflate and cause damage to the lungs or ears if you try to inflate them without a pump.
❖ Do not play with balloons in the kitchen – a balloon may land on a hotplate or ignited gas ring – or near open fires or radiators.
❖ Dispose of burst balloons immediately by putting them in a waste bin.

How to Make Balloon Balls

Balloon balls are easy and fun to make. They are also very colourful. To start your juggling career you will need three balloon balls.

Uncooked rice

Scissors

Small plastic bags

Balloons in different colours

1 Cut the stems off two balloons so that you are left with the round part of each balloon. Fill a plastic bag with 1¹/₂ cups of rice. Seal in the rice by folding the bag around itself.

2 Insert the bag containing the rice into one of the cut balloons. This is a bit fiddly as you have to be careful not to split the bag or the balloon. Do not worry if part of the plastic bag is still visible.

3 Insert the balloon and bag of rice into the second balloon. Make sure the second balloon covers any visible bits of the plastic bag. It does not matter if a part of the first balloon is still visible.

4 Cut the stem off another balloon and cut a few small holes into the round part of the balloon. Stretch this balloon over the balloon ball. Repeat using another cut balloon.

When stretched over the balloon ball, the holes in the outer balloons allow the colours of the balloons beneath to show through. Do not stop now, you have two more balloon balls to make!

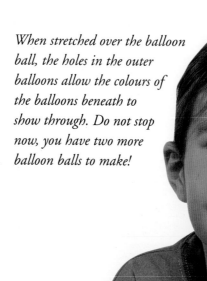

How to Make Bean Bags

Get out your sewing thread and needle, it is time to make a juggler's favourite piece of equipment – bean bags!

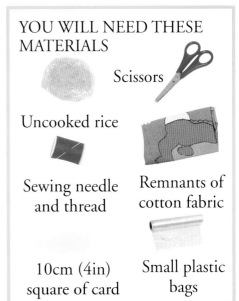

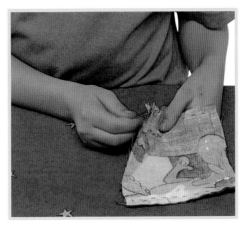

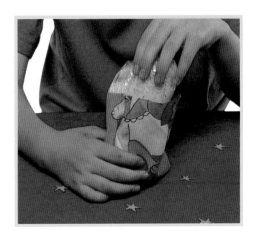

1 Using the square piece of card as a template, cut out two squares of fabric. To make three bean bags you will need six squares of fabric.

2 Place two squares of fabric right sides facing. Thread the sewing needle and tie a knot at the end of the thread. Sew the squares together along three sides. Turn the fabric bag the right way out.

3 Fill the plastic bag with 1 to 2 cups of rice. Seal the plastic bag by wrapping the bag around itself. Place the plastic bag containing the rice inside the fabric bag.

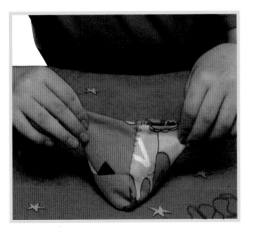

You have now made your first bean bag – only two more to go. Try to use differently patterned or coloured fabric for each one. It will make it easier to follow the movement of each bean bag when you start practising.

4 Fold over the fabric to make a hem around the opening of the fabric bag. Hold the opening so that the two stitched seams touch, as shown, and sew the edges together to make a pyramid.

One-ball Workout

Just like an athlete who has to do warm-up exercises before he or she can take to the track, a juggler also goes through a warm-up workout. These moves will help you to become familiar with the weight and shape of the ball, how it moves through the air and how to anticipate where it will fall. Sounds difficult? Not once you have learned the knack. Do this workout every time before a juggling practice session.

YOU WILL NEED

1 juggling ball, balloon ball or bean bag

Handy hint

This workout can be done using all sorts of objects – sneakers, tennis balls, oranges or even elephants (only small ones, of course!). A good juggler can juggle anything, so now is the time to get in some funny juggling practice.

1 **Clap in time exercise** – this first exercise is really easy. Hold a ball (or small elephant) in your right hand. See, I told you this was easy.

2 Throw the ball in an arc just a little way above your head. While the ball is in the air, clap your hands. Keep your eye on the ball.

3 Catch the ball in your left hand. Now throw the ball from the left hand to the right hand and clap while the ball is in the air.

4 **Under the leg throw** – hold the ball in the right hand and put it under your raised right knee. Throw the ball up, clap and then catch the ball in your left hand. Repeat with the left hand.

5 **Behind the back throw** – hold the ball behind your back in your right hand. Throw the ball up and over your left shoulder. Catch the ball in your left hand. Repeat with the left hand.

6 **Dizzy spin throw** – this exercise tests your balance. Throw the ball up with your right hand. While it is in the air, spin around once. Then catch the ball in your left hand.

7 Repeat the Dizzy Spin Throw, throwing the ball from your left hand to right hand. Spin in the opposite direction. Are you feeling dizzy yet?

The hard workout

Repeat each One-ball Workout exercise five times with each hand. When you can do each exercise without dropping the ball, it is time to move on to the hard workout!

To do the hard workout, repeat the exercises above, but this time throw the ball a little higher and instead of clapping or spinning once, clap three times or spin around twice.

When you can do the hard workout without dropping the ball, do them with your eyes closed. Just joking !

Two-Ball Juggle

Do not panic—two-ball juggling is not as hard as it looks. The secret is to keep your eyes on the balls at all times. Forget about your hands, they are always on the end of your arms. The second part of this exercise is called Juggler's Nightmare. Throwing the balls is easy. The hard part is keeping your hands crossed. Experienced jugglers even find this trick difficult.

YOU WILL NEED

Two juggling balls, balloon balls or bean bags

Handy hint

You can make all these exercises harder by clapping or spinning around while the balls are in the air. If you can do Juggler's Nightmare and spin at the same time, it is time you got a job in the circus!

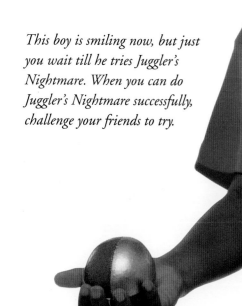

This boy is smiling now, but just you wait till he tries Juggler's Nightmare. When you can do Juggler's Nightmare successfully, challenge your friends to try.

1 Hold a ball in each hand. Throw both balls straight up in the air. Do not throw them too high – just above your head is fine. Catch the balls. Repeat this exercise five times.

2 Stage two of the Two-ball Juggle is to throw the balls so they cross in mid-air and are caught by the opposite hand. Throw one ball a little higher than the other, so they do not collide.

3 For stage three, hold a ball in each hand and throw the balls straight up as in step 1. While the balls are in mid-air, cross over your hands and catch the balls. Try not to go cross-eyed!

4 If you can do this next exercise, you will be juggling three balls within ten minutes. Hold a ball in each hand and relax – this will not hurt a bit!

5 Throw the right-hand ball in an arc above your head in the direction of the left hand. Just as it starts to fall get ready to throw the left-hand ball.

6 Throw the left-hand ball in an arc toward your right hand. Catch the right-hand ball in your left hand, and the left-hand ball in your right hand.

7 **Juggler's Nightmare** – this move is a nasty twist on the one in step 3. Hold a ball in each hand and cross over your arms, as shown.

8 Throw both balls up at the same time so that they cross over and land in the opposite hand. The trick is you have to keep your hands crossed!

9 Catch both balls. Are your hands still crossed? If so, well done. If not, try again. It can take some time to get the hang of Juggler's Nightmare.

Three-ball Frenzy

You had to do it sometime, so grab three juggling balls or bean bags and get ready to perform your first real juggle. You can practise this using scarves if you like. Scarves move more slowly and are easier to catch.

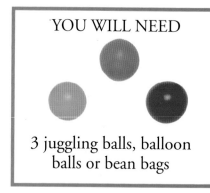

YOU WILL NEED

3 juggling balls, balloon balls or bean bags

Handy hint

Remember to throw the balls straight up, not forwards. If you throw them forwards you will soon be walking all over your audience. You will have enough to do juggling and catching three balls without taking a leisurely stroll at the same time!

This boy has just found out something really important. If he counts 'one, one, one, one' when juggling, it helps him to slow down. Counting 'one, two, three, four' makes you speed up and you know what happens then – all the balls end up on the floor!

1 Hold two balls in your right hand. (If you are left-handed, you may want to hold them in your left hand.) Hold one ball in the other hand.

2 Throw the yellow ball in an arc over your head. Keep your eye on the ball and be ready to throw the turquoise ball when the yellow one starts to fall.

3 At this stage the turquoise ball is in mid-air and you have caught the yellow ball. Throw the red ball when the turquoise ball starts to fall.

4 Catch the turquoise ball but keep your eyes on the red ball that is hurtling over your head. Do not look at your hands when they are catching.

5 You can start to breathe again now for you are about to catch the red ball. Well done – you have successfully completed your first three-ball juggle.

6 **Flashy start** –When you are confident doing steps 1 to 5, try this crowd-pleaser. Hold three balls as in step 1.

7 At the same time throw one ball from each hand straight up. As the balls start to fall, throw the remaining ball in an arc over your head. Keep your eyes on the balls, not your hands.

8 Catch the two balls – one in each hand. When the last ball starts to fall, throw the two balls straight up in the again. Catch the last ball in the opposite hand and then start a normal three-ball juggling routine.

Crazy Juggling

This is a juggling trick for those who really like to perform. You will have to deliver your lines convincingly and look totally embarrassed at the result of your silly trick.

6 bean bags

1 Tell your audience that you are going to do an impression of the world's worst juggler. Hold three bean bags in each hand. Then wriggle your body and move your hands about as though you are readying yourself to juggle. Keep looking upward.

3 As soon as the bean bags land – thud, thud, thud – on the floor, make a desperate face and pretend to be upset. You are, after all, the world's worst juggler!

2 The dramatic movement has arrived – throw all six bean bags in the air. Run about waving your arms in the air trying to catch the bags as they fall. Do not catch any bean bags.

Monkey Juggling

No, you are not going to juggle monkeys, only bananas. This trick is as easy as falling out of a tree, but to make it funny you have to get in some silly monkey business.

YOU WILL NEED

3 bananas or bean bags

1 Place a bean bag or banana under each arm and hold one in your left hand. Cup your right hand. Release the bean bag tucked under your right arm and catch it smoothly in your right hand while making monkey noises.

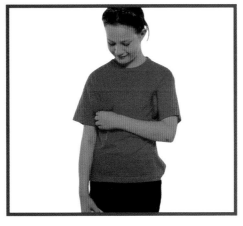

2 While still holding the bean bag in your right hand, tuck the bean bag in your left hand under your right arm. As you bring your left arm down, release the bean bag tucked under your left arm.

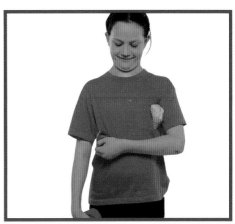

3 Catch the bean bag in your cupped left hand. Tuck the bean bag held in your right hand under your left arm. As you bring your right arm down, release the bean bag tucked under your right arm.

4 Catch the bean bag in your cupped right hand. Now you start the whole routine again. The aim is to practice this so that you become very quick. By the way, did you keep doing the monkey noises or were you just going bananas?

To really get a laugh, start to swing your arms and lope around the stage like a monkey.

209

Under or Over

This time you are going to juggle three balls under your legs and over your shoulders. Whatever next – juggling under water? The important thing with this trick is to raise your leg, rather than bend down. It certainly makes it easier to balance.

YOU WILL NEED

3 juggling balls, balloon balls or bean bags

Handy hint

If you are left-handed, then hold two balls in your left hand and one in your right. Follow the step-by-step instructions, but use your left hand whenever the right hand is mentioned. Likewise, use your right hand when the left is mentioned in the instructions.

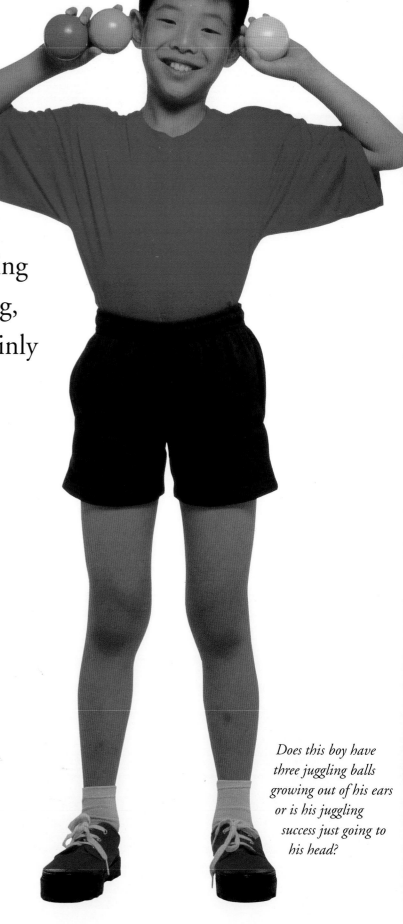

Does this boy have three juggling balls growing out of his ears or is his juggling success just going to his head?

1 **Under the leg juggle** – hold two balls in the right hand and one in the left. Raise your right leg, as shown, and get your balance.

2 Put your right hand under your leg and throw the green ball in an arc toward your left hand. Keep watching the ball.

3 While the green ball is in mid-air, throw the blue ball in your left hand in an arc toward your right hand. Catch the green ball in your left hand.

4 Catch the blue ball in your right hand. Continue juggling normally (see Three-ball Frenzy) except that you will throw the balls from under your leg, not in an arc over your head.

5 **Over the shoulder juggle** – hold two balls in your right hand behind your back. Hold one ball in your left. Look over your shoulder, as shown. Do not stiffen up – try to relax.

6 Throw the yellow ball in your right hand so that it travels upward and then down over your left shoulder. Move your right hand around to the front of your body.

When you become really good at Under or Over, you can do it with juggling clubs. But mind that you do not hit yourself on the head!

7 When the yellow ball starts to fall, throw the green ball in your left hand in an arc toward your right hand. Catch the yellow ball in your left hand.

8 Catch the green ball in your right hand. Now you can commence to juggle in the normal way, except that you will throw balls over your shoulder.

Pampered Pooch

Here we go with your first balloon model. This one should look like a poodle, but do not worry if your first attempt looks more like a bunch of grapes – keep trying!

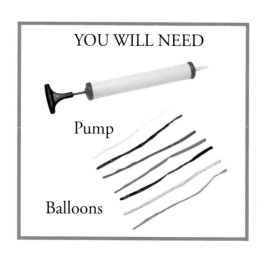

1 Inflate and knot a balloon, leaving 10cm (4in) uninflated at the end. Starting at the knotted end, twist the balloon to make three 8cm (3in) long bubbles. Hold on to the balloon.

2 To form the ears, twist the second and third bubbles around each other. The bubbles are now locked in place. The first bubble forms Pampered Pooch's head and nose.

3 Make three more bubbles slightly larger than the other bubbles. Twist the second and third bubbles around each other to make the front legs.

To make models of other breeds of dog, like the long-bodied and short-legged dachshund, simply alter the length of the bubbles.

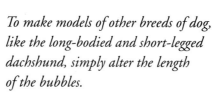

4 Make three bubbles in the other end of the balloon. The first bubble should be 8cm (3in) long, the other two should be slightly larger. Twist together the second and third bubbles to make the hind legs. The bubble nearest the end is pooch's fluffy tail.

Parrot on a Perch

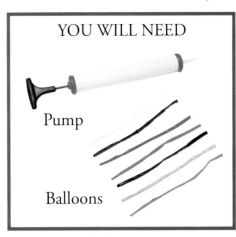

YOU WILL NEED

Pump

Balloons

Polly Parrot is a popular bird! When Polly is not on her perch, you can sit her on your head by putting the loop around your chin. No wonder Polly thinks you are crackers!

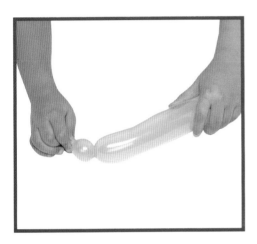

1 Completely inflate a balloon and knot the end. Make a small bubble at the knotted end of the balloon for the parrot's beak.

2 Pull the knot and bubble down beside the rest of the balloon. Twist and lock the knot around the balloon to form another slightly larger bubble. The first bubble is the beak and the second bubble is Polly's head.

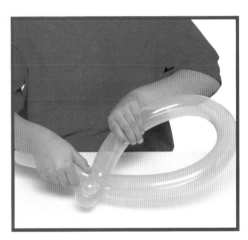

3 You will wonder where the next move is leading, but do not worry, it will soon become obvious. Bend the balloon to form a large loop. Twist the balloon around itself about 18cm (7in) from the end to make the tail.

4 This is the tricky bit, so good luck! Position the tail in the middle of the loop. Pinch and twist the tail and the two sides of the loop together, approximately 8cm (3in) below the head, to make the parrot's body and wings. All you need to do now is arrange Polly on her perch.

This parrot on a perch makes a great decoration. Simply tie one end of a piece of string around the top of the perch and attach the other end to your bedroom wall or ceiling.

Big Elephant

Here is an elephant with a great, long trunk. If you want, you can make the ears bigger and the trunk shorter – it will look just as funny!

YOU WILL NEED

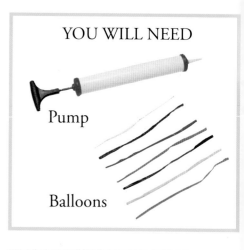

Pump

Balloons

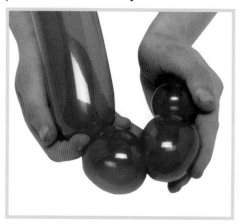

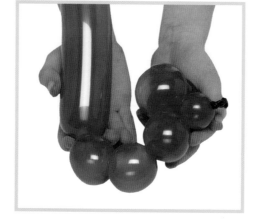

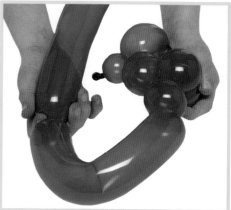

1 To make this balloon model, you start with the tail and work up towards the head. Inflate the balloon, leaving 8cm (3in) uninflated at the end. Knot it. Twist the balloon to make three bubbles, the first 2.5cm (1in) long and the next two 4cm (1$\frac{1}{2}$in) long.

2 Twist and lock the two larger bubbles together to form the back legs. The smaller bubble is the elephant's tiny tail. Make three more bubbles, each 4cm (1$\frac{1}{2}$in) long, for the body and front legs. Hold on to the bubbles until they are locked into position.

3 Twist and lock the end two bubbles to make the front legs. Make two bubbles – one 2.5cm (1in) long and one 11cm (4$\frac{1}{2}$in) long – to make the neck and one ear. Twist the long bubble around the small one.

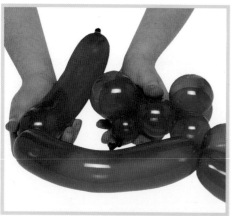

4 Make another 11cm (4$\frac{1}{2}$in) bubble. Twist and lock it around the neck bubble. This is the elephant's other ear. Slightly bend the remaining length of balloon to make the enormous, trumpeting trunk.

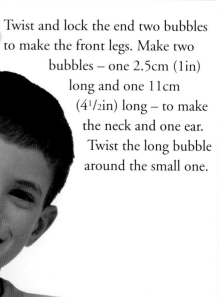

214

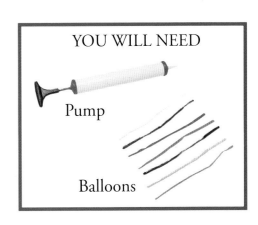

Tiny Mouse

YOU WILL NEED

Pump

Balloons

Did you know that elephants are terribly frightened of mice? Funny to think that something so enormous and strong could be scared of something so tiny and cute.

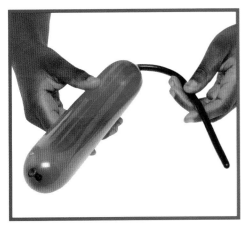

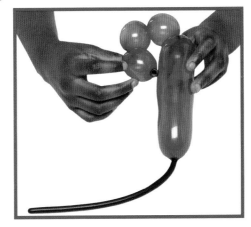

1 To make a tiny mouse, you only need a tiny balloon, so inflate only the first third of the balloon. This will leave the balloon with a long uninflated tail. Tie a knot in the end.

2 To form the head, twist three small bubbles each 4cm (1½in) long. Twist and lock the second and third bubbles together to make the ears. The first bubble forms the head and nose.

3 Twist three small bubbles of the same size to make the neck and front legs. Twist and lock the second and third bubbles as before. See, balloon modelling is easy!

4 Can you guess what comes next? That's right, three more small bubbles! Twist and lock these to form the body and back legs. The rest of the balloon is the mouse's long tail.

Make a family of tiny mice using different coloured balloons.

King of Hearts

This smart crown will make you look like the King of Hearts. You do not have to add a balloon to the top of your crown, but why not? You could add a heart-shaped or round balloon, or even some bits of ribbon. Go on and make a crown fit for a king—or queen.

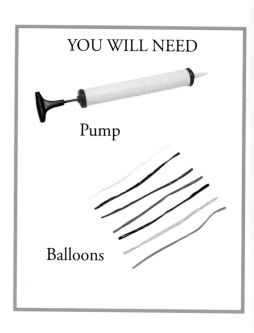

YOU WILL NEED

Pump

Balloons

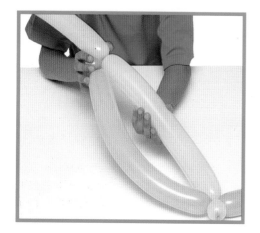

1 Fully inflate two balloons and knot the ends. Twist the balloons together, as shown, to make a headband. The free ends of both balloons should be the same length.

2 Find the midpoint of the free end of each balloon. Twist the two balloons together at the midpoints.

Why not have a balloon hat-making contest to see which of your friends can create the wackiest hat?

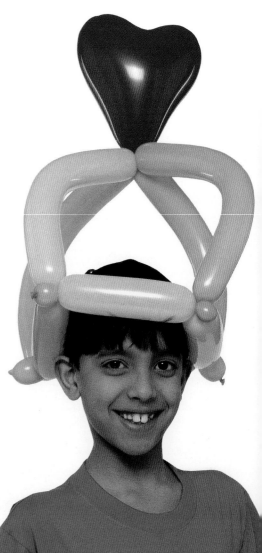

3 Make a small bubble in the end of one free end. Twist it around the headband, halfway along one side.

4 Make a bubble in the other free end. Twist it around the headband, halfway along the opposite side. All loyal subjects should now bow to the king!

Dashing Sword

This Dashing Sword looks great, but it is not much chop at cutting anything. At least you and your friends will not hurt each other during mock battles! Make a scabbard by joining two balloons together and wearing them around your waist.

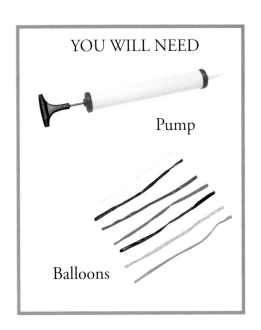

YOU WILL NEED

Pump

Balloons

1 Inflate a balloon, leaving 5cm (2in) uninflated at the end. Knot the end. Push the knot inside the balloon about 4cm (1½in) and hold it in position. Use your other hand to squeeze the balloon around the knot. Twist the balloon to hold the knot in place.

2 Twist the balloon to make two bubbles. The first bubble will form the handle. The second, longer bubble will form one third of the shield that protects the hand. Bend the longer bubble, then twist and lock it around the first bubble.

3 Twist the balloon to make another third of the protective hand shield. Twist and lock it around the handle, as before. If you make the hand shield bubbles too long, your Dashing Sword will be really short!

Balloon swords burst very easily, so make your sword fights really gentle or be ready to make lots of swords.

4 Make the final part of the hand shield in the same way.

Crazy Balloon Tricks

Impress and amuse your family and friends with these brilliant balloon stunts. You must never tell anyone the secrets of how to do the tricks!

You are bound to be asked to repeat these tricks, so have a few balloons prepared.

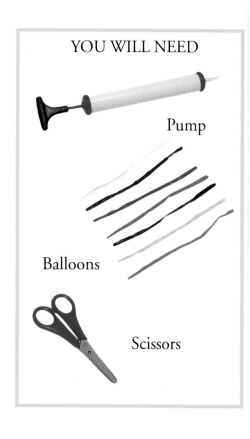

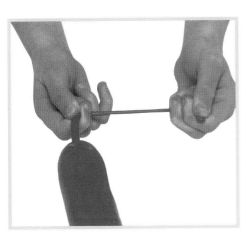

1 **Appearing bubble** – to prepare for this trick, inflate a balloon and leave 18cm (7in) uninflated at the end. Knot the balloon. Grip the uninflated section with both hands, as shown. Now stretch the balloon. Go on, really pull!

2 To perform the trick, show the audience that it is an ordinary balloon. Twist a bubble 5 to 8cm (2 to 3in) long at the end of the balloon and hold it in your hand. The audience should not see you do this.

3 Tell the audience that you will make a bubble appear at the end of the balloon. Without the audience seeing, squeeze the bubble really hard. A small bubble should magically appear at the end of the uninflated section.

4 **Magic balloon** – to prepare, take two uninflated balloons of the same colour and cut the end off one of them with a pair of scissors. Slip the cut-off end on to the end of the whole balloon.

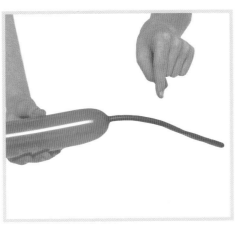

5 Tell your friends you have a magic balloon and offer to show them a trick with it. Inflate the balloon, but leave the end uninflated. There needs to be a space between the real end of the balloon and the false end.

6 Hold the inflated end of the balloon with one hand, and the false end with the other. Say to your friends that the balloon is too long and that you are going to make it shorter. Pull sharply on the false end.

7 Your friends will not understand why the balloon has not deflated.

Practise and prepare

It is important that you practise and prepare these tricks before you perform them in front of an audience. It is also a good idea to work out exactly what you are going to say.

Do not forget that some of the moves in these tricks are not meant to be seen by the audience.

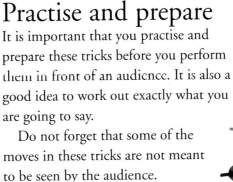

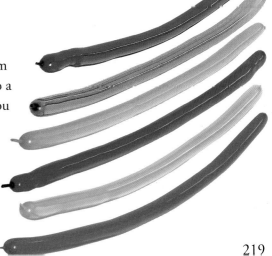

Bunch of Tulips

What a beautiful bunch of tulips! These balloon flowers last longer than real tulips and they do not need watering! You could tie a big, colourful ribbon around the stems to make a lovely present.

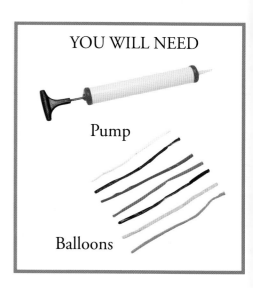

1 Inflate only 8cm (3in) of one balloon, leaving a very long uninflated section. This will be the stem of the tulip. Knot the end. Hold the two ends of the inflated section of the balloon, as shown.

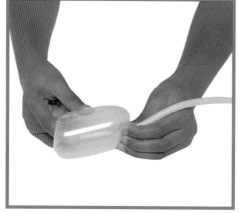

2 Use your finger to push the knot into the balloon until the knot reaches the other end of the inflated section. This will take a little bit of practice, so do not give up after the first attempt.

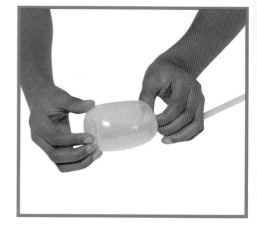

3 Take hold of the knot with the other hand. Remove your finger from inside the balloon. While holding the knot very firmly, twist the balloon several times. This will hold the knot in place.

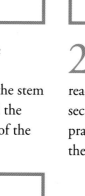

4 Now that you have made one beautiful tulip, go on to make a whole bunch in different colours.

If you want to be really cunning, you can make the tulips stand up by inserting thin plastic straws inside the balloons before you inflate them.

Sunflowers

Just like real sunflowers, these balloon sunflowers are enormous! But unlike the real ones, they will not turn their colourful heads to face the Sun. Make two or three and use them to decorate your bedroom.

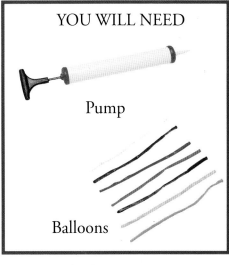

YOU WILL NEED

Pump

Balloons

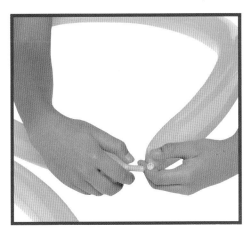

1 Inflate two balloons, leaving only a very short uninflated end in each one. Knot the ends. Tie the knotted end of each balloon to the other end to form two circles.

2 Now for a bit of fun and a lot of squeaking. Twist each circle to make a figure 8 shape. Both ends of the figure 8 should be the same size.

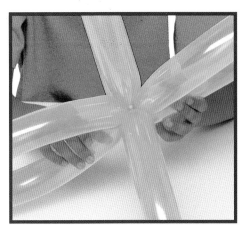

3 Twist the two figures of 8 together to make a cross. These are the gigantic petals of your sunflower. Let us hope there are no gigantic bees or caterpillars about.

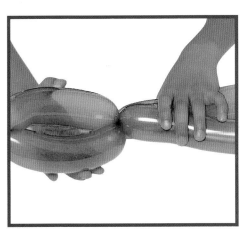

4 Inflate another balloon, once again leaving only a small uninflated end. Twist a loop in the centre of the balloon. Twist another loop next to the first one. These are the leaves and stem.

To finish, insert the end of the stem balloon through the centre of the petals. Twist the stem to lock it in place.

Building a Balloon House

This house is a great favourite and it is really fun to build. Use your imagination to add extra rooms or to make balloon doors, windows, trees, lamp-posts and furniture. Make it as big as you like, but remember that your house will not be very warm in winter and you will get soaked when it rains!

This balloon house is multi-coloured, but you could make your house using red balloons for the walls and black balloons for the roof.

1 Inflate 17 balloons and knot the ends. Seventeen balloons is enough to build this one-room house, but for grander designs you will need more balloons. Twist the ends of four balloons together to make a square. Make another square in the same way.

2 Use four more balloons to link the two squares together and make a cube. Twist the ends of the balloons to lock them in position. Is it time for a tea-break yet?

3 Attach a balloon to each top corner of the cube. Twist the end of two balloons together to make a triangle. Do the same with the other two balloons. To finish the roof, link the triangles with a balloon.

4 Well done! You have built a home you can truly call your own. Now is the time to work out ways of adding extra rooms or making your house a little more private.

Pop! goes your dream house

Before you start constructing your house make sure that the floor beneath it is smooth and free of splinters or sharp edges. Sadly, your dream house will collapse if the balloons are punctured. It might be a good idea to cover the building site with an old sheet before you start inflating the balloons.

Once you have built your first house, go on to create other types of houses. This one is called the Wonky Tepee model!

Magic Fun
and Sneaky Tricks

Nick Huckleberry Beak

Introduction

To put on a really amazing magic show you need to know the three Ps. No, not three garden peas, but the three magic Ps – preparation, presentation and performance. You can forget all about that abracadabra mumbo-jumbo, just remember the three Ps.

Preparation

To avoid getting halfway through a wickedly good trick and realizing that you are missing a vital piece of equipment, you must be prepared. You must have everything you will need at your fingertips. The only way that you can be properly prepared is to make a list of the items that are required for each trick. As you gather them together, tick them off the list. Simple idea, but it works. Have you made your list yet? No, then get to it!

Presentation

This is all about how you dress and act in front of your audience. Presentation is very important if you want your magic show to be a great success. To find out more about presentation read Magical style.

Performance

You have decided to put on a show. Congratulations! First thing you must do is work out which tricks you will do and the order you will do them in. There are no rules for this, but remember that a short show full of knock-out tricks is better than a long show with only a few good tricks.

This trick is in the bag (or should that be envelope?) because this girl has everything prepared.

The best way to give your magic show atmosphere is to use music. Try to match the speed and mood of the music to the pace and style of your act. If you are doing lots of quick tricks, use fast music. If your show is spooky and full of shocking surprises, find a piece of really creepy music.

If you do not use music then you will have to write a script and rehearse the words you are going to say. You may want to introduce each magic trick or tell a little story about where you learned a certain trick. But whatever you say, it is a good idea to have prepared it. It also never hurts to have a couple of good jokes up your sleeve. These can be used to entertain your audience while you get your next trick ready. Do not use any bad jokes – only I am allowed to use them.

Magical style

Even if you can do some of the hardest magic tricks in the world, your show might flop if your presentation style is dead boring. To be a big hit with an audience you have to have pizzazz, you have to have style. Problem is, you cannot buy pizzazz in a supermarket (I tried once and came out with two frozen pizzas instead), but you can learn the tricks of great presentation.

Make a big show of displaying empty hands or objects to your audience. It will distract them from seeing what you are really up to!

This boy has magical style. He is smiling, wearing his favourite hat and looks ready to take a big bow.

Dress style

The traditional costume for a magician is a smart suit, bow tie and flashy cape. Nowadays almost any sort of costume is fine. A colourful waistcoat and a pair of jeans can look just as smart and professional. If you want to work out your own wacky costume, go ahead. My rule is – if you feel good, you will look good.

Stage style

To be a show-stopping performer, you must know the secrets of the trade. The first is, always enter from the side or from the back of the stage. Then walk to the middle, smile at your audience and wait for the applause.

The second thing to do is introduce yourself to the audience. You can use your own name or invent a colourful stage-name.

Number three is always to face your audience. This will mean that your props, or equipment, will have to be within easy reach. Your audience have not come to watch you rummage upside-down in a box.

The fourth trade secret is this – if you make a mistake or a trick does not work, try to laugh it off. You can even pretend that the mistake was meant to happen. Then you can do the trick again, but this time do it correctly.

My last tip to you is this – let the audience know you have finished a trick by taking a small bow. Save the big bow until the end. As soon as they see you bow, the audience will clap and call out for more.

Entertaining style

This one is easy to explain. If you have a smile on your face and look as though you are enjoying what you are doing, the audience will also enjoy themselves. Try to look confident and relaxed. When you talk to your audience, speak clearly and loudly. No one will hear your great jokes if you mumble and mutter.

Professional style

If the audience ask you to repeat a trick or to tell them how it was done, refuse politely. If you tell all your secrets, you will have to learn a whole new routine, and a trick is never as good second time around.

Sometimes it helps to look as surprised as your audience.

Materials

These are some of the main materials and items of equipment you will need.

Carbon copy paper When placed between two sheets of paper, inky side down, it will copy whatever is written on the top sheet of paper.

Coloured and white paper and card For many of the projects, you can recycle pieces of paper and use card from cut-up cereal boxes. Large sheets of card can be bought in stationery shops and craft shops.

Marker pen A marker pen is a type of felt-tip pen that draws quite thick lines. If you do not have a marker pen, use an ordinary felt-tip pen instead.

Paperclips A good collection of paperclips is vital for any promising magician.

PVA glue This is a strong glue that can be used to stick together paper, wood or even fabric. It can bought in stationery shops and is sometimes called craft glue or white glue. You will need a brush or glue spreader to apply the glue.

Recycled boxes For the projects in this book, you will need two empty boxes – a large one and a small one. A cereal box and a small tea or chocolate box would be ideal.

Rubber bands These are almost as important to the budding magician as paperclips. You can buy bags of assorted rubber bands in stationery shops.

Ruler Accurate measuring is required for some projects so you will need a ruler divided into centimetres (cm) or inches (in).

Safety scissors Safety scissors are smaller than cutting scissors. Their edges are rounded and the blades are not as sharp as normal scissors.

Sticky-back plastic This plastic material comes in many colours and designs. It is usually bought in rolls. To make it adhere to a surface, you simply peel off the protective backing and press the sticky-back plastic on to the object.

String It does not matter if you use plain or coloured string as long as you have lots of it.

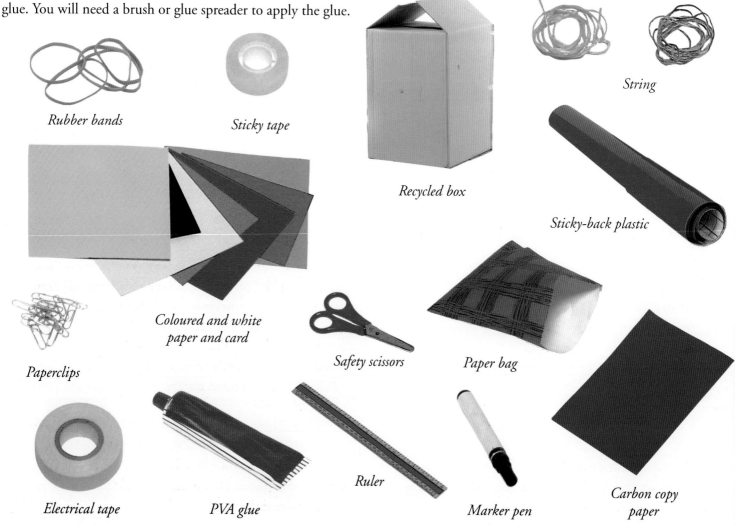

Rubber bands

Sticky tape

String

Recycled box

Sticky-back plastic

Coloured and white paper and card

Paperclips

Safety scissors

Paper bag

Electrical tape

PVA glue

Ruler

Marker pen

Carbon copy paper

Equipment

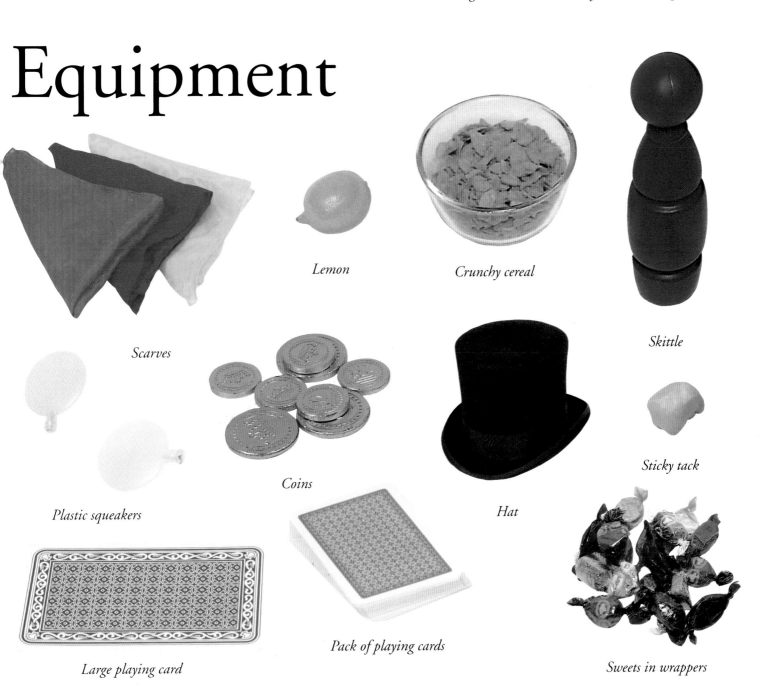

Lemon

Crunchy cereal

Scarves

Skittle

Coins

Sticky tack

Plastic squeakers

Hat

Large playing card

Pack of playing cards

Sweets in wrappers

Coins You can use real or plastic toy money when practising or performing tricks. You will need five coins.

Crunchy cereal Use a breakfast cereal made of large, crunchy flakes. Ask permission before raiding the kitchen!

Hat All magicians have got to have a hat – your audience will expect it! It can be a dashing top hat, a favourite baseball cap or even a crazy sunhat.

Large playing card This is about four times the size of a normal playing card. You can buy it in joke shops and toy shops.

Lemon You can use a real or plastic lemon to do the Magic Box trick.

Plastic squeakers These are round, plastic discs that squeak when squeezed. You can buy them in joke shops and toy shops. They are not expensive.

Playing cards A pack of playing cards consists of 52 cards plus two jokers. There are four suits – hearts, diamonds, clubs and spades – numbered from ace to king. There are two black suits and two red suits. To do all the tricks you will need two packs of cards. Playing cards are inexpensive and can be bought in toy shops and stationery shops.

Scarves You can use large or small silky scarves or handkerchieves. Brightly coloured or patterned ones are best.

Skittle This is used when playing indoor or garden bowls. It is made of plastic.

Sticky tack This reusable material is used to fix posters on to walls. You can buy it in packs in stationery shops.

Sweets in wrappers You will need quite a few sweets wrapped in foil or cellophane. Do not start eating them before you have completed the trick!

Missing Money

This trick is every magician's favourite. Why? Because it cannot go wrong. All you need are five coins and some sticky tape fixed to the palm of your hand. Keep the palm of your hand hidden throughout the trick, otherwise the audience will work out your secret.

Handy hint

In place of a loop of sticky tape you can use a small piece of double-sided tape. Use small coins rather than large ones – large coins are harder to conceal and too heavy to adhere to the tape. You can use plastic coins if you like.

YOU WILL NEED THESE MATERIALS

5 small coins of the same size

Strong, clear sticky tape

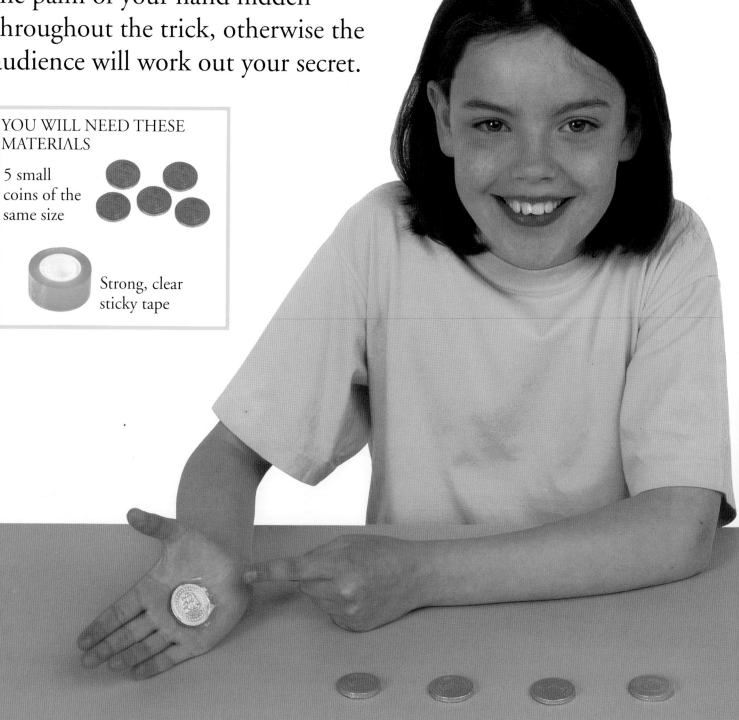

1 Cut a small piece of sticky tape about 5cm (2in) long. Overlap the ends, sticky side out, to make a loop. Place the five coins in front of you on the table.

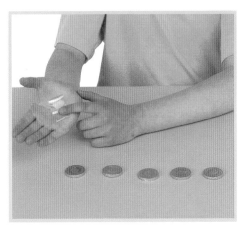

2 Firmly press the loop of tape on to the palm of your hand. Do not let anyone see you doing this. This little bit of magical sneakiness is just between you and me.

3 Make a big show of counting the five coins one-by-one as you stack them neatly one on top of the other. Ask your audience to count along with you.

It is a secret!

In this trick, the missing coin remains missing. You do not reveal where you have concealed the fifth coin. Remove the coin and sticky tape from your hand discreetly while you are returning the other coins to your pocket or to your magic box.

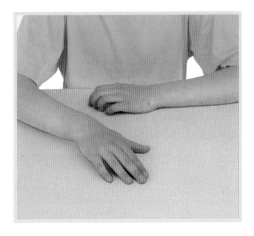

4 Press the hand with the sticky loop on to the pile of coins. Say your chosen magic words and then withdraw your hand. The top coin will be stuck to the loop.

5 Keep the palm concealing the coin flat on the table. With the other hand, spread out the pile of coins and count them out loud. Yikes! There are now only four coins.

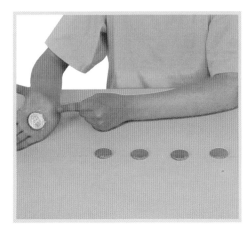

6 The fifth coin, of course, is still stuck to your hand.

Tricky Tubes

This is another classic trick that is used by magicians everywhere. It involves moving a handkerchief from one 'magic' tube to another tube to give the impression that both tubes are empty. In the finale of this trick you stun the audience by producing a handkerchief from the empty tubes.

YOU WILL NEED THESE MATERIALS

2 pieces of different coloured card 30cm x 30cm (12in x 12in)

Rubber band

Small handkerchief

9 paperclips

1 Steps 1, 2 and 3 show what you have to do to prepare for this trick. Roll the pieces of card to make tubes. One tube must be narrower so that it will fit inside the larger tube. Secure the tubes with eight paperclips.

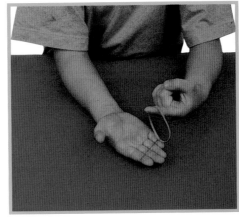

2 The device that makes this trick work is a paperclip. Unfold the paperclip to make hooks at either end, as shown. Attach a rubber band to one hook. Roll up the handkerchief and thread it into the rubber band.

3 Hook the other end of the paperclip on to the top of the narrow tube. The rubber band and the handkerchief will be on the inside of the tube. Make sure that the handkerchief is totally hidden from view.

4 Now it is time to get this show on the road! Hold up the large tube so that the audience can see that it is completely empty. This should not be difficult as it really is empty!

5 Pick up the narrow tube and slide it slowly down through the large tube. As you do this the paperclip holding the handkerchief will hook itself on to the large tube.

6 Pull the narrow tube out from the bottom of the large tube. Then, with a flourish, hold up the narrow tube to show your audience that it is empty.

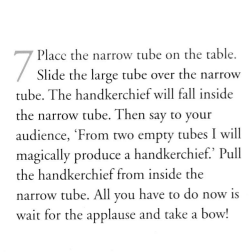

7 Place the narrow tube on the table. Slide the large tube over the narrow tube. The handkerchief will fall inside the narrow tube. Then say to your audience, 'From two empty tubes I will magically produce a handkerchief.' Pull the handkerchief from inside the narrow tube. All you have to do now is wait for the applause and take a bow!

Magic Box

The Magic Box can produce objects out of thin air. One minute the box is empty, the next it is not. Only you know about the secret box that can hold a lemon, a pack of cards or even an elephant. If you are going to pull an elephant out of the box, perhaps this trick should be called the Magic Trunk!

Practice makes perfect

To get this trick right takes lots of practice. You should be so familiar with it that the audience are not even aware that you turn the box around in step 8. One wrong move and the lemon (or the elephant) will come tumbling out for all the world to see! To make this trick really impressive, ask someone in the audience to lend you their watch, wallet or sunglasses. Their mouth will drop when they see their object disappear and then reappear.

YOU WILL NEED THESE MATERIALS

1 small recycled box

1 large recycled box

Sticky tape

Ruler

Scissors

Marker pen

PVA glue

Lemon

Sticky-back plastic

1 To make the Magic Box, tape the ends of the boxes closed. Cut the top off the small box. Use the marker pen and ruler to draw a line along one long and two short edges of the large box.

2 Cut along these lines carefully to make a hinged lid on the large box. By the way, did I tell you to empty the boxes before you started this project? Oops, oh well!

3 Do the same to the other side of the large box but this time the hinged lid is on the opposite edge. You must get this right or the Magic Box will not be very magical.

4 Tape, glue or nail the small box securely to the inside of one of the hinged lids. (Forget nailing – I was just joking.) The opened top of the small box must face where the lid is hinged.

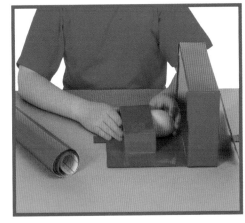

5 Cover the box with sticky-back plastic. Cut two strips of plastic to make tabs. Fix tabs to the outside edge of the lids, fold in half and fix to the inside edge. Put the lemon in the small box.

6 Now it is magic time! Place the box on the table. The lid containing the small box is on the bottom with the tab nearest you. Hold on to both tabs because you are about to open the box.

7 Raise the box and pull on the tabs to open both lids. Say to your audience, "This box is empty – but not for long." Lay the box on the table.

8 The lid containing the lemon should be on the bottom. Turn the box around, hold the tab and lift the lid. Hold up the lemon to the audience.

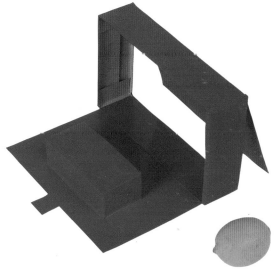

The Big Picture

So that you can say hello or farewell to your audience in a magical way, I have prepared this special trick. It is a very simple illusion where a small picture suddenly becomes a big picture. Carefully follow the instructions for folding the paper, or you will be saying hello or goodbye to yourself.

YOU WILL NEED THESE MATERIALS

Marker pen

2 sheets of paper

PVA glue

Scissors

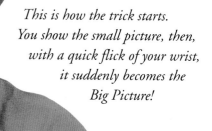

This is how the trick starts. You show the small picture, then, with a quick flick of your wrist, it suddenly becomes the Big Picture!

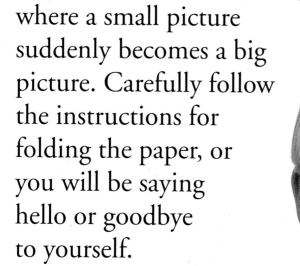

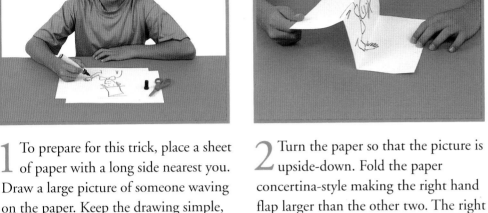

1 To prepare for this trick, place a sheet of paper with a long side nearest you. Draw a large picture of someone waving on the paper. Keep the drawing simple, you will have to repeat it later.

2 Turn the paper so that the picture is upside-down. Fold the paper concertina-style making the right hand flap larger than the other two. The right hand flap is on the bottom, as shown.

3 Fold the paper away from you, so that the top flap is a little smaller than the bottom flap. I know this sounds complicated, but it is easy. I could not do it if it was too hard.

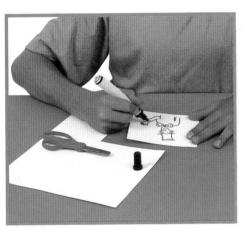

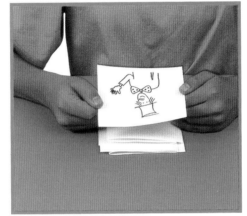

4 Take the other sheet of paper and cut out a rectangle that is exactly the same size as the bottom flap of the folded paper. On to this rectangle, draw the picture that is on the folded paper.

5 Glue this picture on to the front of the large flap. The bottom of the picture will be nearest the fold. (See, I told you this is easy!) Apply the glue carefully so that it does not spread on to the other flaps. You are ready to present the Big Picture.

6 Hold the paper, as shown, with the fold at the bottom and the small drawing facing the audience. To stop the paper unfolding, support the flap with a little finger. Tell the audience that you are going to give them a cheery welcome or a sad farewell wave.

7 Quickly pull sideways so that the folded paper unfolds and the big picture is revealed.

Before their very eyes, the audience have seen the small picture become a great, big picture. If you have been an ace magician and practised this routine lots of times, then your audience will be totally taken in by the illusion. In place of a drawing you could write a message, like "Welcome to the Greatest Show on Earth!"

The Big Card Trick

You may have seen this trick performed many times, but now you will be able to do it yourself. You can choose any number or suit you want for the large playing card, but a card of the same number and suit must be at the top of your pack of playing cards. The two cards fixed to the large card must be numerically smaller than the big card.

Handy hint

You can make your own large playing card with stiff white card and a black marker pen. It does not matter which suit or number you choose to draw, as long as it is the same as the top card on your pack of cards.

YOU WILL NEED THESE MATERIALS

Pack of playing cards and 1 large envelope

Sticky tack

Large playing card

1 To prepare for this trick, use a small piece of sticky tack to fix a two and a four of any suit on to the back of the large ten of clubs card. Place them in the envelope. Also check that the ten of clubs is the top card on your pack of playing cards. Now let the show begin.

2 Invite someone from the audience to join you on stage and cut the pack of cards. No, not with a pair of scissors. To cut the cards, all your guest has to do is take a pile of cards off the top of the pack and lay them beside the remaining cards.

3 Place the bottom half of the pack on top of the other cards. Place it so that it is at right angles to the cut cards. This will show you where the pack was cut and where you will find the ten of clubs. Tell your guest that they will shortly see their secret card.

4 Remove the upper stack of cards from the pile and turn over the next card. Without looking at the card, show it to your guest. Tell them that they must remember what their secret card is. You know that it is the ten of clubs!

5 Ask your guest to shuffle the cards as much as they like. When they are shuffled, you can put them into the envelope. This envelope contains the large ten of clubs card plus the two other smaller cards.

6 Tell your guest that you are going to find their secret card. Put your hand into the envelope and pull out the two card. Ask if this is the secret card. They will say no. You then ask, 'Is it bigger than this?'

7 Repeat the routine as in step 6, but this time pull out the four card. It is now your big moment to astound and amuse everyone. Put your hand into the envelope again and pull out the large ten of clubs card. Show it to your guest and say, 'Is this big enough?' You have shown your guest that you knew that their chosen card was the ten of clubs all the time.

Double Envelope Trick

To make sure that 'Top Secret' documents sent by post are not read by the wrong person, use the Double Envelope Trick. This sneaky envelope has a hidden compartment that only you and your friend will know about. If anyone else opens it, the envelope will appear empty. To fool snoops, put a false message into the envelope.

YOU WILL NEED THESE
MATERIALS

Two large identical
envelopes

Scissors

Paper
glue

1 Cut the front, including the flap, from one of the large envelopes. Trim a little off the edges of the cut section of envelope.

2 Slide the cut section of envelope inside the other envelope. The flaps on both envelopes should line up. So far, so good!

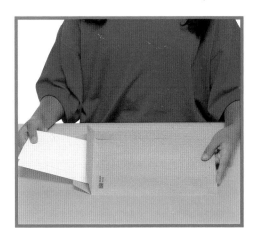

3 Place the secret message into the envelope, sliding it into the opening between the two flaps. Have you ever seen anything so sneaky?

4 Paste the two flaps together with paper glue. This will seal the hidden compartment that contains the message.

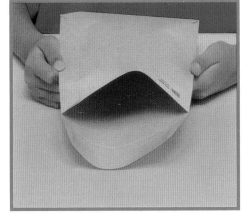

5 If the envelope falls into the wrong hands and it is opened, the envelope will either be empty or contain a false message. The snoopy sneak will be very disappointed or totally confused!

6 You and your friend know exactly what to do with the Secret Envelope. Simply lift up the glued flap and rip it off. Slide a hand inside the now opened hidden compartment and pull out the 'Top Secret' message.

7 The envelope must have contained some surprising news judging by the look on this girl's face.

There are only two snags to the successful use of the Double Envelope Trick. Firstly, it does not work with bulky items like books or gifts. And secondly, you and your friend have to be discreet when preparing and opening the envelope. Never open the envelope where there are prying eyes or your secret will be out of the bag – or should that be out of the envelope!

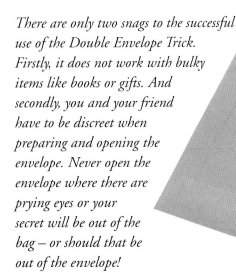

See the Unseen

Here are two techniques for seeing the unseen—reading messages that you were never intended to read. For the first method you have to get hold of the notepad quickly.

YOU WILL NEED THESE MATERIALS

Notepad

Wax crayon

Carbon paper

Scissors

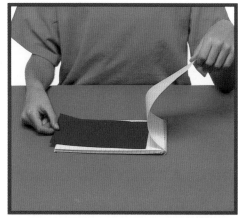

1 **Method 1**—Get the notepad on which the torn-out message was written. Rub the crayon gently over the top sheet. The impression made by the written message will remain unshaded.

2 **Method 2**—To intercept a message, trim a sheet of carbon paper so that it is smaller than the notepad. Turn over two pages of the notepad and insert the carbon paper ink side down.

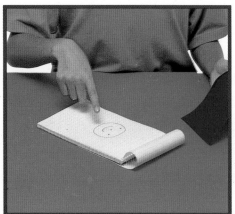

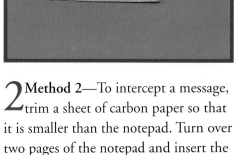

3 Once the message has been written and the person is out of sight, turn the top pages of the notepad over and remove the carbon paper. On the page below will be a copy of the message. Take care doing this and never attempt to intercept truly personal messages.

Noisy Alarms

Crunch, crackle, pop, squeak! What are those noises? They are the sounds of your bedroom security devices going noisily into action. I bet the intruder got a surprise!

YOU WILL NEED THESE MATERIALS

Crunchy cereal

2 plastic squeakers

Handy hint

You will have to keep changing the positions of your alarms or they will prove ineffective against intruders.

1 **Noisy warning 1**—This may sound a little odd, but crunchy cereal makes a great nighttime alarm. All you have to do is leave a pile of cereal just outside your bedroom door.

2 When the unwitting intruder steps on the cereal, you will hear the crunch, crackle and pop! The intruder will realize that their sneaky game is up and will run away.

3 **Noisy warning 2**—In case the intruder misses the crunchy cereal alarm, place one plastic squeaker under a rug near the door and another under the cushion of a chair. (Even intruders have to sit down sometime!) Now all you have to do is wait.

When you hear the squeakers "squeak" you will know that you have not caught a mouse, but a sneaky rat!

Trick Wallet

Open one flap of this wallet and it is empty. Open it the other way and – wow! – there is the secret document. Make two identical Trick Wallets so that you and a friend can switch wallets (and secret information) without being detected. When using the wallet to play a trick on someone, distract his or her attention so that they do not notice you turning the wallet over.

Handy hint

If you are going to use your Trick Wallet as part of a magic act, the wallet should be quite large. This will make it easier for the audience to see what is and what is not happening. When using the wallet for secret messages, make sure it will fit easily into a pocket.

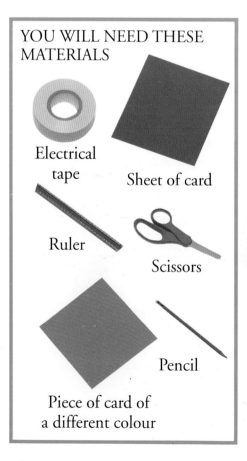

YOU WILL NEED THESE MATERIALS

Electrical tape

Sheet of card

Ruler

Scissors

Pencil

Piece of card of a different colour

1 Measure and draw three rectangles, each 20cm x 8cm (8in x 3in) on to the sheet of card. Cut out the rectangles. You can make a big wallet by cutting out three larger rectangles.

2 Lay the rectangles side by side and join the edges with electrical tape, as shown. The tape should act like a hinge, allowing each piece of card to fold over easily.

3 Tape the joins on the back of the card and fix electrical tape along the remaining two short sides. Position the tape so that it can be folded over to the back to give a neat finish.

4 Concertina-fold the wallet, as shown. Lay the wallet on to the table and gently press it flat.

5 To test the Trick Wallet, place a small rectangle of the other coloured card between two of the flaps. Close the flaps. Turn the wallet over and open the flap. If the flap is empty you are doing the right thing. Close this flap.

Magic trick wallet

To make the wallet work in a magic show routine, you have to be discreet when turning the wallet over so that your audience does not catch on to the trick. The only way to achieve this sleight of hand is to distract them by making a funny face or telling a joke. A good magician always has (among other things!) a couple of good jokes up his or her sleeve.

6 Turn the wallet over again and open the flap. If all has gone to plan, the flap will contain the piece of card.

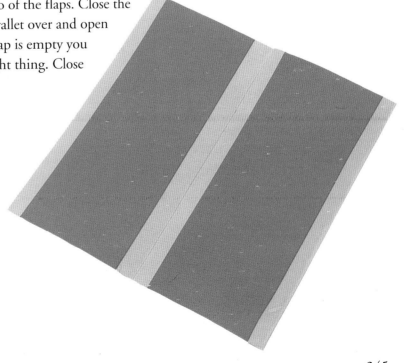

Candy Disguise

Everyone has heard about sending messages in bottles, but only you and I know how to pass on vitally important messages inside candy wrappers. There is only one problem with Candy Disguise—resisting the urge to eat the candy. If you eat the special candy and discard the wrapper, your message will remain a secret forever.

Handy hint

It is not a good idea to conceal your message inside the wrappers of sticky candy—your message will be forever stuck to the candy. The best types of candies to use are chocolates. Yum, yum!

YOU WILL NEED THESE MATERIALS

Pencil or pen

Sheet of paper

Scissors

Tape

Paper bag

Candies in wrappers

1 Cut out a piece of paper no larger than the wrapper on the candy. Use this to write your secret message on.

2 Unwrap one of the candies and lay your message on the inside of the wrapper. Do not eat the candy—yet!

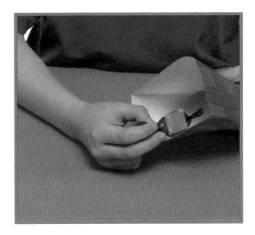

3 Place the candy on top of the message and the wrapping paper. Rewrap the candy.

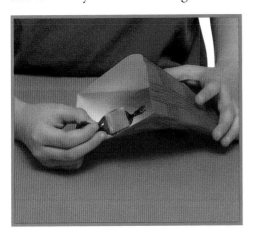

4 Make a loop from a short length of tape. The sticky surface should be on the outside of the loop. Stick the loop to the candy and then press the candy to the inside of the paper bag. Attach it about halfway down the bag.

5 Carefully put the rest of the candies in the bag, making sure that you do not dislodge the special candy. Your secret message is now safe. No one will suspect that you are carrying vital information inside a bag of candies.

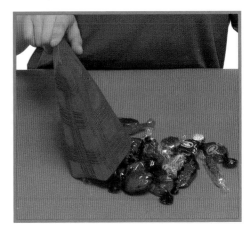

6 When you are ready to pass on the secret message to your best friend, all you have to do is empty the bag. You can even ask your other friends if they would like a candy. Not only are you clever, you are also very generous!

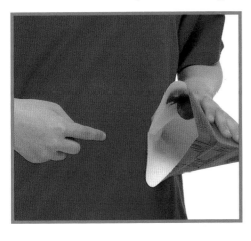

7 See, your secret message is safe! It is still stuck to the inside of the bag. Offer your best friend this candy. He or she can eat it, while reading your note.

Once you have delivered your message safely, you can relax. It is also time for you to have a candy. Now, which one will you choose?

247

Joke in the Post

Want to send someone a shocking surprise?
All it takes is paper, paperclips and sticky
tape. Joke in the Post is
so easy to assemble
that you could make
one for each of your
friends. But will they
still be your friends
after you have played
this joke on them?

YOU WILL NEED THESE MATERIALS

1 small envelope

Sticky tape

Sheet of paper or thin card

2 small rubber bands

3 paperclips

Marker pen

1 Fold the sheet of paper or thin card into equal thirds. Press the folds flat with your hands and then open out the paper again.

2 Open out two paperclips to make L-shapes, as shown. Bend and shape another paperclip to form a circle. Do this carefully – the ends are sharp.

3 Tape the L-shape paperclips to the paper and loop rubber bands around the ends, as shown. Thread the rubber bands on to the wire circle.

4 Slowly wind the wire circle around and around. The rubber bands will twist and tighten. Whatever you do, do not let go!

5 Re-fold the paper without letting go of the wire circle. Carefully insert the folded paper into the envelope and seal it.

6 Address the envelope using the marker pen. Post or deliver the envelope to your friend.

7 When your friend opens the letter the rubber bands will unwind causing the wire circle to spin and clatter against the paper. This is bound to make your friend jump in fright.

Handy Signals

Getting messages to friends can be tricky when you are involved in a hush-hush surveillance operation or working in the library. So instead of shouting messages, use hand signals. On the next page are examples of just a handful (ha, ha!) of hand signals and their meanings. Use them alone to convey a simple message or link them together for more complicated instructions. When you have mastered these signals, go on to invent your own.

YOU WILL NEED

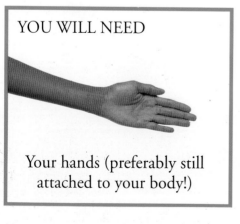

Your hands (preferably still attached to your body!)

1 **Quiet!**—Press a finger to your lips when you want someone to stop talking. Move the finger over to your ear to say "listen."

2 **Yes and no**—Resting your chin on a hand with the thumb pointing up means "yes." To say "no," point the thumb down.

3 **Danger warning**—Place a hand loosely around your throat to warn friends that the situation is dangerous and to take care.

4 **Come here**—Running a hand through your hair from the front to the back means "come here."

5 **Go away**—Hiding your face behind one hand means "go away." Use two hands to say "go away quickly."

6 **Look**—Placing a finger next to the right eye means "look right." A finger next to the left eye means "look left." Fingers next to both eyes means "look straight ahead."

When you have mastered these signals, go on and invent your own. But before you forget what each new signal means, write it down.

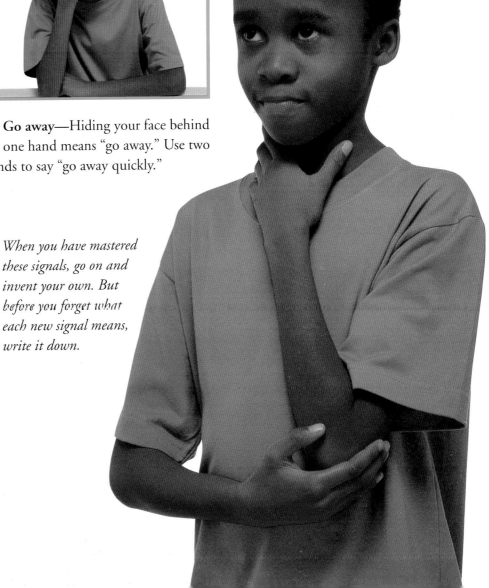

Final Challenge

Your mission is to rescue the skittle from the circle using only string and a rubber band. You and your accomplice cannot enter the circle, nor touch the skittle. The only bit of floor the skittle can touch is the area on which it is standing. Good luck!

YOU WILL NEED THESE MATERIALS

Scissors

Rubber band

Balls of string

Plastic skittle

The Final Challenge is not easy, but that makes it all the more challenging. Now it is time to put your thinking caps on – there is a poor damsel skittle in distress that needs to be rescued.

1 Draw a circle 1¹/₂m (48in) in diameter using the chalk. (A hoop is used here for clarity). Place the skittle in the middle of the circle. Cut four lengths of string 2m (2yd) long.

2 Thread lengths of string through the rubber band. The rubber band should be midway along each string. Hold the ends of the strings, as shown.

3 Gently pull on the strings to stretch the rubber band so that it will fit easily over the top of the skittle. Lower the rubber band over the neck of the skittle.

4 Allow the rubber band to tighten around the skittle by relaxing your pull on the strings. Carefully raise the skittle out of the circle. Do not pull on the strings as this will loosen the rubber band's grip on the skittle.

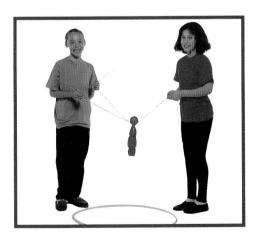

5 Congratulations, you have done it! Now see if your friends can do it.

This is a great game to play at a party. To make it more difficult for your friends, you can set a time limit in which the challenge must be completed.

Index

Acknowledgements

The publishers would like to thank the following children for modelling for the craft projects – Nana Addae, Richard Addae, Mohammed Adil Ali Ahmed, Charlie Anderson, Lauren Andrews, Steve Aristizabal, Joshua Ashford, Emily Askew, Rula Awad, Nadia el-Ayadi, Nichola Barnard, Michael Bewley, Gurjit Kaur Bilkhu, Vikramjit Singh Bilkhu, Maria Bloodworth, Leah Bone, Chris Brown, Cerys Brunsdon, William Carabine, Kristina Chase, Chan Chuvinh, Ngan Chuvinh, Emma Cotton, Charlie Coulson, Charley Crittenden, Lawrence Defraitus, Vicky Dummigan, Kimberley Durrance, Holly Everett, Alaba Fashina, Terri Ferguson, Kirsty Fraser, Fiona Fulton, Nicola Game, George Georgiev, Lana Green, Liam Green, Sophia Groome, Laura Harris-Stewart, Lauren Celeste Hooper, Mitzi Johanna Hooper, Briony Irwin, Kayode Irwin, Isha Janneh, Rean Johnson, Reece Johnson, Sarah Kenna, Camille Kenny-Ryder, Lee Knight, Nicola Kreinczes, Kevin Lake, Victoria Lebedeva, Barry Lee, Kirsty Lee, Isaac John Lewis, Nicholas Lie, Alex Lindblom-Smith, Sophie Lindblom-Smith, Claire McCarthy, Erin McCarthy, Elouisa Markham, Laura Masters, Mickey Melaku, Imran Miah, Yew-Hong Mo, Kerry Morgan, Jessica Moxley, Aiden Mulcahy, Fiona Mulcahy, Tania Murphy, Lucy Nightingale, Ify Obi, Adenike Odeleye, Laurence Ody, Folake Ogundeyin, Fola Oladimeji, Ola Olawe, Lucy Oliver, Yemisi Omolewa, Kim Peterson, Mai-Anh Peterson, Josephina Quayson, Pedro Henrique Queiroz, Alexandra Richards, Leigh Richards, Jamie Rosso, Nida Sayeed, Alex Simons, Charlie Simpson, Antonino Sipiano, Marlon Stewart, Tom Swaine Jameson, Catherine Tolstoy, Maria Tsang, Frankie David Viner, Sophie Louise Viner, Devika Webb, Kate Yudt, Tanyel Yusef.

Gratitude also to their parents and Hampden Gurney School, Walnut Tree Walk Primary School and St John the Baptist C. of E. School.

The authors would like to thank the following for their assistance in providing materials and advice –Boots; Dylon Consumer Advice; Head Gardener, Knightsbridge; Lady Jayne; Mason Pearson, Kent; Molton Brown; Tesco. Special thanks to Justin of Air Circus; 'Smiley Face' from Theatre Crew, Tunbridge Wells; and the Bristol Juggling Convention.